"The messa
autistic peo

Laurie M

The Journey

Approaching Autistic Adulthood

The Road Less Travelled

Grace Liu

Approaching Autistic Adulthood

First published in 2021 by

Panoma Press Ltd
48 St Vincent Drive, St Albans, Herts, AL1 5SJ, UK
info@panomapress.com
www.panomapress.com

Book layout by Neil Coe.

978-1-784529-57-4

A CIP catalogue record for this book is available from the British Library.

This book is available online and in bookstores.

Dedication

To autistic people across the spectrum who know how lonely autism can be in a neurotypical-dominant world, and to the neurotypicals who listen and stand by us.

Dear Nicky,

Thank you for such a wonderful retreat and for all your advice on my career choices. It has been a pleasure to get to know you!

Best wishes,

Grace

Testimonials

"The message Grace's book brings to autistic people is: you're not alone."

Laurie Morgen, author of *Travelling by Train – The Journey of an Autistic Mother*

"It's best to learn from autistic adults. Grace's book shows there's always more to learn about autism and yourself!"

Thomas Henley, YouTuber at Aspergers Growth

"Grace's authentic writing reminds us that experiences that sometimes feel alienating are what make us beautiful and unique."

James Pratt, host of Silent Superheroes podcast

Acknowledgements

To my parents Helen and John. Thank you for fighting for my diagnosis and for getting me through years of isolation, miscommunications with neurotypicals, and struggling to accept myself. Thank you to Mum for getting me through a parental divorce and moving countries and for raising Rhian and me on your own for as long as you did. Thank you to John for becoming a full-on dad to us, helping out with studies and various life skills, and for helping me with the practicalities of this book, despite "being an awkward bastard about it at this stage" (your words, not mine).

To my sister Rhian. Thank you for your support of my endeavours, your tough love, and all the wacky childhood anecdotes we have shared. Also, thank you for your unintentional but major role in my childhood development – always needing me to play with you so that I had to learn how to interact with neurotypical children!

To all my extended family. Thank you for all the support you've shown me and my work, no matter the distance.

To my university mentor Laurie. Thank you for getting me through my first year at university, for all your support since and for helping me as much as you have with this book.

To all the other autistic adults who have contributed their anecdotes to this book. Thank you for agreeing to be a part of this and for inadvertently helping me feel less alone in my experiences.

To the friends I have specifically mentioned in this book. Thank you for all the anecdotes I have written about and for all the ones I haven't. Special thanks to my friend known in the book as Lizzie for playing such a key role in my coming out journey.

To my Creative Writing and Journalism lecturers from university. Thank you for helping me get my writing skills off the ground.

To Kev, my hairdresser. Thank you for giving me a much-needed post-lockdown haircut just in time for my back cover photo.

To Deb, Bernard, Hester, James, and family. Thank you for your hospitality, support and for treating me as one of your own.

To Charlotte. Thank you for all the laughs we shared at work and for understanding autism better than any other neurotypical person in the company.

To Lucy, Chris, Rooster, and Nelly. Thank you for sharing your house with me for a year.

To Ann, my mentor during my internship. Thank you for seeing me through a very socially demanding year.

To Alicia, my second-year college LSA (Learning Support Assistant). Thank you for all your support at college and for getting back in touch with me over the past couple of years and for supporting my work since.

To all my cats, past and present. Thank you for years of companionship and laughter and for not holding me to neurotypical human standards.

Last but definitely not least, to Mindy, Emma, and the rest of the team at Panoma Press. Thank you for your faith in my writing, for answering my many questions about the publishing process, and for publishing this book.

Contents

Introduction

How I came to write this book

When I was nine, my parents (my mother and stepfather – they married the previous year) had something to tell me after years of me misunderstanding my classmates' social rules. We had moved into my stepdad's house in a different town, and I was enrolled at a school where my struggles were spotted with the eyes of a hawk. This was a sharp contrast to my previous school, where nobody seemed at all curious about why I constantly misunderstood the social rules my classmates picked up effortlessly. And now, I was facing a diagnosis.

Something called Asperger's Syndrome, on the autistic spectrum. Something which meant I was made a little bit differently from other kids. Something which meant I would be given extra help at school from now on.

I remained silent for a moment. I had some thinking to do. Then I asked outright the question that was uppermost in my mind, "Can I have a piece of cheese?"

Let's go back a few years. I was born on 17th March 1993 – bang on my due date – in Taipei, Taiwan. From England, UK, my mum was working as a dancer in Taiwan, having graduated from ballet school. My father, from Taiwan, was a bouncer at a club where my mum worked for a while, and within a few years, they were married. My early memories of my parents fighting and Mum locking herself and me in their bedroom are testaments to how badly it went. A few days after I turned four, and three months before my sister was due to be born, Mum took me and got on a plane back to England. We moved in with my grandparents, my sister was born, and within a year, we were living in a Housing Association flat, where we stayed until Mum married my stepfather.

My mum knew I was different pretty early on. Maybe starting from the day my kindergarten teacher in Taiwan tried to teach us how to make clay pots, and I decided to make penguin feet instead. Or a couple of years later, during 'African week' at school, when we'd been given African bags to draw on, and I drew a snowman on mine.

But my differences could have been put down to any number of circumstance-driven reasons. In Taiwan, I was half English, being raised knowing two cultures. In England, I was half Taiwanese, living in a single-parent family, having lost contact with my biological father, and left everything that was familiar to me. Mercifully, I was oblivious to my teachers telling my mum I was 'odd', 'slow', and 'strange'. And to other children's social rules. And to the fire alarm going off while I was engrossed in a particularly captivating piece of writing... Until my diagnosis.

What has life been like for you growing up? It might have been hard. Maybe you were bullied. Maybe you had to deal with family conflict. Were you that kid who drifted through the early years, unaware of how other people saw you, with a tendency to slip under the radar? As you may have guessed, I was definitely an 'under-the-radar' kid. To begin with, anyway.

Since my school years, I have been to both college and university, with two years of home study in between. I have studied diverse subjects, including animal management, journalism, and creative writing. I have been employed, unemployed, and done voluntary work in animal care and journalism. I have encountered challenges of many kinds, some positive and some negative. I have moved out of the parental home and (largely thanks to the coronavirus pandemic) back in again. I have explored my religious faith and had varied experiences of church. I have had to deal with assumptions about my mixed-race heritage as well as my autism. More recently,

I have opened up about my sexual orientation, something I am still learning to accept.

So I can say with conviction that the transition from adolescence to adulthood is a challenging time. Loads of new social rules come into place, and it seems like everyone is fighting their way to the top of the social hierarchy. Your brain and body have changed and are still changing. The same applies to the dynamics in your relationships. And then, just when you think you've conquered it all, everything changes again. Suddenly you face a lifetime of having to create your own world, and not have it organised for you. Pretty scary, huh? I can't lie; it is. But you can and will find the capacity to face it with a strong support system and a good understanding of your own goals and abilities. As a 28-year-old who has been blogging about autism since 2013 (at unwrittengrace.wordpress.com), I'm still figuring it out. So let's figure it out together and look at a few common struggles.

The aims and content of this book

I have aimed to make this book relevant and useful to you if you fit one or more of the following descriptions:

- You are an autistic person getting used to, or aspiring towards, an independent adult life.
- You are an autistic person who wants something relatable to read.
- People assume you need minimal help or understanding because, to some extent, you can manage your own life, yet you feel like you spend your whole life masking your natural traits.
- You have been made to feel as though your strengths and potential don't matter just because your abilities and communication are very different from neurotypicals'.

- You are an older adult with autism, and you wish that books like this existed when you were younger.
- You are an autistic person who wants to make sense of the neurotypical world.
- You think you might be autistic.
- You are a neurotypical person who knows someone who fits any of the previous points and wants to understand them a bit better.
- None of the above points are relevant to you; you're just curious.

If any of this sounds like you, please keep reading!

Most of the anecdotes and advice I have included are my own, but I have also used quotes from other autistic adults to back up some of the points I have made and to give a broader scope of how autistic people may experience certain situations. Their contributions have been highly valuable to me and are an enlightening read. The following people have given me permission to disclose their identities:

- Laurie Morgen – my first-year university mentor, author of *Travelling by Train – The Journey of an Autistic Mother*, and public speaker.
- Thomas Henley – YouTuber at *Aspergers Growth,* host of the *Thoughty Auti* podcast, creator of *Asperger's in Society* documentary, and Taekwondo champion.

The other contributors wish to be kept anonymous and will be known as:

- Abby
- Naomi

- Kathleen
- Will
- Luna

I must also acknowledge the fact that the phrase "the road less travelled" comes from Robert Frost's poem *The Road Not Taken* (1920). I did not know this until shortly before submitting this book for publication. You really do learn something new every day!

Throughout this book, you will see the word 'neurotypical' come up a lot. This is the technical term for a non-autistic person. When talking about autism, I will mainly use 'identity-first' language (i.e. 'autistic person') because that's what most autistic people prefer. However, I will occasionally use 'person-first' language (i.e. 'person with autism') for the sake of others on the spectrum who prefer that. I'm mentioning this because I am aware that this is a controversial topic. In casual conversation, I don't mind if people use a combination of both, but if I had to strictly adhere to one, I would choose identity-first language. When talking to another autistic person in real time, if they express a preference, I will respect it and go with it either way. Personally, though, it annoys me when neurotypicals try to make the rules about this. Insisting on person-first language implies a negative bias as if autism is something to be ashamed of, which is an attitude I'd rather leave in the past.

Another thing I steer clear of these days is the word 'symptoms' when talking about autism. In this book, I will instead say 'signs', 'characteristics', or 'traits'. Although people (including some on the spectrum) commonly use the word 'symptoms', they also use it when talking about illnesses. And I am very firm about not counting autism as an illness.

I know the term 'Asperger's Syndrome' is less commonly used than it was when I was diagnosed, due to Hans Asperger's association with the Nazi regime. I will say 'Asperger's Syndrome' when talking about my diagnosis or early experiences because that is what I was diagnosed with, but I will say "autism" most of the time.

You will notice that at the end of the book, I have included a glossary of metaphors and idioms to clarify any obscure figures of speech. Make as much or as little use of this as you wish. It's there because I realise that the meaning of some expressions frequently used by neurotypicals can be very unclear to autistic people.

Right. I think I have set the scene. On to the first chapter.

CHAPTER 1

Explaining Autism

What is autism?

There is a lot of confusion surrounding autism, and with confusion comes stigma and misunderstanding. People often think of it as a male condition, or a childhood condition, or a white person condition. They might assume we are Einstein-level geniuses, or the complete opposite, when actually most of us fall anywhere in between. They might think we don't have feelings or don't care about other people just because we don't express ourselves in a neurotypical way. I have often heard it said that this stereotype, combined with the assumption that we are technology-obsessed geniuses, makes us sound like robots. Hence the picture on the previous page of a robot on one side, and bookish, oversensitive, cat-loving me on the other! And if we don't come across as obviously autistic, people just think we are shy, introverted, perfectionistic or 'quirky'.

Right, there's my rant on what autism isn't. So what exactly is it? For those of you who think you might be autistic or who know someone who is, I'll do my best to summarise.

First and foremost, autism is characterised as being a difference in communication. This in itself can mean many things. For a start, some autistic people are non-speaking. Some speak a little. Some speak fully. Some find their ability to speak varies depending on their wellbeing. Most of us find ourselves at odds with neurotypical communication to some extent. We often communicate more literally and logically than neurotypicals and are less reliant on body language, facial expressions and unspoken implications. Many of us struggle with eye contact. As a result of all of this, neurotypicals often see us as inexpressive and therefore unemotional.

Something else that perpetuates this stereotype is the fact that autistic people sometimes struggle to identify and process emotions. This is called alexithymia, and I have learned about it only recently. I used to think it didn't apply to me because I feel emotions very strongly and am very sensitive to other people's. On reflection, though, I have realised that although I am usually aware of my emotions, I often find it hard to put them into words because they feel too complicated and too abstract for me to do that. Not knowing how to describe our feelings doesn't mean we don't have them. Neurotypicals, please take note!

One trait that autistic people are known for is intense interest in a certain subject. Some interests become a chosen study or career path, some simply remain a long-term interest, and some may be fleeting. My longest lasting interest would be cats. When we develop an interest in something, we have a strong urge to find out as much as we can. We may love talking in detail about the subject and be able to remember everything we know about it with little effort. If we do choose to pursue our favourite subject as a study or career path, we often do so single-mindedly and with great dedication.

Another common feature of autism is a difference in how we experience sensory stimuli. I'll be touching upon this topic several times, but I'll summarise it here first. Compared to most neurotypicals, we are often over-sensitive or under-sensitive to certain stimuli. Thomas Henley, YouTuber at *Asperger's Growth,* cannot stand certain types of light. I have always been sensitive to touch and sound. I often cannot help reacting to sudden touch or touch from someone I don't know well. I prefer gentle, moderate physical affection, unlike my friend Will who loves a tight, prolonged bear hug! I can clearly hear a harmony in a song I'm listening to but am also easily overwhelmed by too much background noise. My friend Kathleen has a strong aversion to certain foods, as depicted in this rather graphic quote:

> *"I am a very fussy eater and am disgusted by certain food types – the look, the smell, the texture. For instance, being around people eating baked beans is a real challenge for me. I would honestly rather eat a worm than a baked bean, which says a lot coming from a vegetarian!"*

This reminds me of how I compare mushrooms to slugs. Sometimes it's the gory analogies that get the message across.

Many people on the spectrum also show signs of dyspraxia, i.e. difficulty with gross and/or fine motor coordination. You could argue that this is another sensory issue. Gross motor skills, such as sport, dancing, and getting around on slippery or uneven ground, have always been difficult for me. On the other hand, fine motor skills, such as drawing, writing, and making things, are among my main strengths. Thomas is the complete opposite. He is less into creative tasks that require a steady hand but is a leading Taekwondo champion, something that I could never hope to achieve!

A common feature of both autism and dyspraxia is executive dysfunction or trouble with executive functioning skills. These skills include things like concentration, working memory, multitasking, motivation, and flexible thinking. When I am faced with a big and/or unfamiliar task, it can take ages for me to make any progress if I don't know exactly what I'm aiming for or what I need to do to get there. I have often been chided in situations like that for not taking more initiative when very often I'm just daunted by not knowing what to do.

In short, it's hard to accurately summarise autism because it means something slightly different for each person. What I want people to understand is that while most autistic people will share some traits, we are a pretty diverse group. Sadly, there are a lot of negative stereotypes about autism, but do not let this fool you into thinking being autistic is inferior to being neurotypical. It is just different, and in a world designed by and for neurotypicals, being different can be pretty disabling. It took me a long time to be ok with it and accept it as a part of my identity. If this book can help some of its autistic readers reach that point, I will be happy!

Coming out of the autism closet

Throughout primary school, I was dimly aware that I was different from everyone else, though I couldn't describe it. I spent most of my time alone. I had intense interests. Some of my classmates were unkind to me. Despite all this, I lacked the self-awareness and awareness of others to really dwell on it, and initially, my diagnosis didn't change that.

Secondary school was a different world altogether. Suddenly children were less accepting of a kid whose favourite conversation starter was "I know all about cat breeds." Secondary school teachers were less understanding than their primary school counterparts. I had a timetable and – worse – lesson locations to memorise. I seemed to make friends, and then had no idea what to do when things went wrong with them. In short, I was vulnerable and all too aware of it.

So from then on, I learned to hate the fact that I was different. I tried hard to form friendships and often failed. As a result, I was afraid to talk about autism to anyone because I knew I didn't communicate well and was scared of being judged. I even compared telling people about it with talking about periods to a boy! And because they didn't understand why I was different, people thought I was weird, stupid or – and I quote – 'boring'. Needless to say, I don't miss that time in my life.

A few years later, things slowly changed. I got invited to a social event and made friends with Will, who appears a few times in this book. He took me aside and talked to me about his own Asperger's diagnosis and how he had learned to accept it, which prompted me to do the same. I wasn't ready to open up to everyone but held on to that day, nonetheless. Several months later, something similar happened after church, when someone empathised with my difficulty with socialising because they had Asperger's. I began to talk about my own struggles, and from that day, I was able to explain to people about autism whenever the subject of social struggles came up in conversation.

I wasn't expecting to talk about it on either of those occasions. But when I did, it made me realise that there are people who know what it's like and people who want to learn. It also made me realise that I did not want to spend my whole life not talking about such a key part of myself due to fear of being judged. To avoid that, I would have to overcome that fear and step out of my comfort zone.

I have come to realise that I am not alone in having felt like this. Autistic people, as with people in any minority category, are so often conditioned to see their differences as a bad thing. When your differences aren't immediately obvious, it can add to that fear of how people might react if they knew. I think this is something that many autistic people struggle with at some point. I certainly did, and so did my friend Kathleen:

> *"I remember telling my close friends that I was autistic and breaking down into tears. I felt I was revealing this huge secret. I was scared they would look at me differently, but it was fine. They didn't know much about autism at the time, so they just had the 'that's cool. You're still you' response."*

How to tell people depends on the situation. If you are struggling to socialise in a place with lots of people and someone is trying to understand and help you, you can say, "I am autistic, which makes it hard for me to read neurotypical people and understand social interaction with them." Or "I am autistic, which means I have very sharp senses, and all this noise and background activity is really uncomfortable for me." You may also want to talk about it when it comes up naturally in conversation, either because the person you are talking to mentions autism directly or because they mention something relevant, such as other disabilities or social struggles. While you may have to deal with certain misunderstandings surrounding autism, most people these days will not reject you or react with hostility. If they do, that will hurt, but it will also prove that they are not someone you want in your life.

> *"My advice to others would be not to do what I have done in the past and hide autism. Pretending to be neurotypical is exhausting and generally not very convincing anyway!"*

My friend Naomi's experience and advice in the previous quote pretty much mirror my own. I have gone from seeing autism as a shameful secret to being tired of not being able to be open and real with other people. My first-year university mentor Laurie Morgen makes some valuable points about the importance of self-acceptance:

> *"You are who you are, and the worst thing in the world is to fight it. Self-acceptance is so important on many levels, and the two most important ones, in my opinion, are 1) your mental health matters above and beyond other people's opinions of you; 2) others seem to pick up on it when we're not being genuine, and it causes alienation. If we know who we are and shake hands with that person, it's the start of self-acceptance."*

When anyone asks me to summarise what autism means for me, I give the following points:

- Difficulty in reading faces and body language
- Prone to misinterpreting what people say, e.g. long, complicated instructions
- Poor physical skills
- Reasonable IQ (not Einstein-level, but satisfactory)
- Detailed long-term memory
- Good with written and spoken language

Then there are big events where it is important for anyone in charge to understand you and your strengths and weaknesses. This is where a longer explanation in writing may be necessary. When I was 23 and had just left university, I got an internship working at a Christian bookshop for a year. This was a Christian internship, so I was enrolled on a weekly church discipleship course with other Christian interns. To begin with, it was stressful. How many times have you spent the day in a new place full of strangers who you are encouraged to make friends with? It's not easy, is it?

Three weeks later, with our first weekend away approaching, I was beginning to wonder if I would ever enjoy these sessions. I still didn't feel like I knew anyone well, and yet our leader at the time put so much emphasis on how important it was to connect with each other. I know phrases like 'be vulnerable', 'be open', or 'go deeper with one another' came with the best of intentions, but honestly, it wasn't long before I would break into a cold sweat at the sound of them.

To make it worse, the upcoming weekend included outdoor group activities and as much bonding time with each other as we were willing to spend. In other words, more vulnerability and openness, plus a bunch of games that set an autistic, dyspraxic person up for failure. I had just about had it with the course at this point.

But I was determined to make the best of the year. At my parents' suggestion, I wrote the following letter to give to our leader and anyone else who might be interested. Neither the weekend nor the course was perfect, but I learned a lot, had fun, and ultimately got through the year despite its challenges.

> *Hello,*
>
> *I'm writing to explain what Asperger's Syndrome means for me. Asperger's tends to be less obvious than other forms of autism. I am gentle and articulate and communicate best through writing. I'm looking forward to getting to know people and would really like to get the most out of being a part of this community.*
>
> *My main struggles include social interaction, physical coordination, and taking in lots of information from different sources or with a lot of distractions. In a group setting, I struggle to keep up with what's going on. I may either keep asking or lose focus altogether. It helps if*

someone discreetly updates me on things I need to know, one to one. I am more likely to understand instructions/explanations that are a concise summary of the main points rather than too much detail. I like being on top of schedules, so I hope I don't seem pushy if I keep asking what is going to happen.

Lively group situations can be overwhelming, and I don't present myself at my best when I don't know anyone. I tend to be more at ease and outgoing with a close friend. Once I am used to people, I am cooperative, friendly and motivated. I am better at mingling than I was, but I still sometimes drift towards the edge of the group without trying. I also find it hard to remember names and faces at first – just bear with me when this happens.

Despite this, I do want to connect with people. I try very hard to treat others well and care deeply for my close friends. Contrary to the autism stereotype, I am empathetic and intuitive to people's emotions. It's on-the-spot, face-to-face interaction I find harder. It's not that I don't want to be with you personally; it's just that I often need time to myself.

Being autistic means that I show signs of dyspraxia (impaired physical coordination). I'm good at long walking, running, and lifting heavy objects but have more trouble with team games, walking on uneven or unstable terrain, and learning directions. My fine motor coordination is much better, meaning I am good at using my hands for small, precise tasks.

I know this sounds like a lot, but apart from where specified, I don't expect anyone to do anything drastically different. Usually, I just want others to understand and be patient. When in the right place (literally and figuratively), I am intelligent, mild-mannered, witty, and a deep thinker, and I hope that I can make friends and contribute to the fullest.

Hope this helps and thank you for reading!

Grace

It's tricky trying to explain the way you are and have always been. It's like trying to explain your own accent to someone. For you, it's the norm, no matter how strange it sounds to the other person. To explain how you are different from another person, you first have to have an objective understanding of both perspectives. When neurotypicals ask what it's like to be autistic, it sometimes feels like they're assuming you know what being neurotypical is like in comparison. If you are unsure how to answer, consider explaining the following: what do you do that others apparently don't? Or vice versa? What do you find easier than most people? Harder?

One of the annoying things about being autistic is that not only do you have trouble knowing how to communicate with neurotypical people, but also they don't always know how to communicate with you. Because of this, I have taken much time to learn how to explain myself and my needs in a way that is easy for neurotypicals to understand and to learn and adapt to neurotypical communication. Life would be much easier if more neurotypicals put that much effort into autism-friendly communication.

Meanwhile, neurotypical-written autism resources continue to say that autistic people have poorer social skills than neurotypicals. I'll save a rant about that particular issue for another day.

Dealing with people's reactions

People often seem to forget that there are many different ways to be autistic. A common reaction in neurotypicals when being told about autism is to reply with questions and statements loaded with assumptions, such as 'People with autism always…' or 'Does that mean you're very…', or 'Ah, like Rainman (or another overly stereotyped autistic fictional character)'. As if they know more about autism than me. Hence a recently coined term 'Neurotypical-splaining' – when neurotypicals needlessly explain autism to an autistic person. I came up with this term myself but have since come across it elsewhere, so clearly, I'm not the only one to think of it.

NT-splaining may seem innocent enough, and I'm well aware that generally, people who do this mean well. They probably don't know how to respond and are trying to continue the conversation. But, as an autistic person, I can't help finding it annoying. If what they say is accurate, then they are pointing out something that is obvious to me. If it is inaccurate, then it sounds ignorant.

As suggested by Laurie, I came up with a table of things people sometimes say when you talk about autism and possible ways to reply if they are making you uncomfortable. An obvious solution would be to just ignore what they say and carry on talking or change the subject. However, many uncomfortable reactions do not come with ill intent but from a well-meaning person making a mistake due to lack of knowledge. Such a mistake, just like any other, will be easier to correct with patience and clarification than with frustration. Whether you say anything or not is up to you, but if you feel a response is necessary, there are plenty to choose from here. The first couple of points are Laurie's (though I altered the humorous response for the first one), and the rest are mine. You may want to come up with your own additional ideas.

How you can respond

People might say	**Factual response**	**Humorous response**	**Deflection response**
You don't look autistic.	Autism doesn't have a particular "look".	Well, autistic people tend to have a head, hair, two eyes, and four limbs, so I guess I do.	What am I supposed to look like? OR What do you think autistic people typically look like?
Aren't autistic people supposed to be good at maths/ IT/science?	That's just a stereotype – not all autistic people are the same, and I'd like people to get to know me as an individual.	I'm clearly the exception.	What makes you say that?
Oh, I'm so sorry.	Autism isn't an illness; there's nothing wrong with me.	I'm not!	Why are you sorry? (Perhaps follow this up with the factual response).
You can't be autistic because...	Not all autism traits are applicable to every autistic person. OR There are many different ways to be autistic.	Tell that to the person who diagnosed me.	How many autistic people have you met?

We're all a little bit autistic.	While everyone sometimes does something/ has personality traits associated with autism, that doesn't make someone autistic.	Everyone puts on weight sometimes, but that doesn't mean we're all a little bit pregnant.	In what way are we all a little bit autistic?
Ah, like *Rain Man/* Christopher in *The Curious Incident Of The Dog In The Night-time/*(any other overly stereotyped fictional autistic character).	Those characters are strongly stereotyped and not a relatable representation of most real-life autistic people.	Nope, like me!	Is that book/ film/TV show supposed to be an autism diagnostic manual?
It's because of vaccines.	Actually, that was a conspiracy theory from years ago that has been disproven.	Well, I'd rather be autistic than dead!	Are deadly diseases really worse than having a slightly different brain? OR Do you think people are better off dead or seriously ill than being like me?

Don't worry; it's not obvious.	There's no shame in autistic traits being obvious. OR When you're outnumbered by neurotypical people, you have no choice but to learn how to communicate with them. Not because there's anything wrong with autism being obvious, but because people think there is.	I'm not worried whether it's obvious or not.	What's wrong with it being obvious?
But you seem so normal/ you could be normal if you tried.	"Normal" is a subjective word – what's "normal" for one person isn't necessarily "normal" for another.	I am normal – for me, anyway.	What do you mean by normal?
You can get treated/cured/ healed for that you know.	Autism isn't an illness, and actually, many "treatments" for autism cause a lot of psychological damage.	But there's nothing to treat/cure/ heal.	Do you think there's something wrong with the way I am? OR Why do I need to be treated/ cured/healed?

You shouldn't label yourself.	Actually, having a name for being the way I am has helped me understand why I'm a bit different, instead of just thinking I'm stupid or weird.	Well, it's a label that's not going away.	Why shouldn't I have a name for the way I am?
Don't say, "autistic person", say "person with autism". Your condition doesn't define you.	I prefer to say "autistic person". OR I don't have a preference either way. (Either way, maybe follow up with the deflection response).	Perhaps I should also stop calling myself a man/woman and instead say "person with male-ness/ female-ness."	Why should non-autistic people dictate how autistic people talk about autism?
You're lucky to have a job/ an education/ friends/a partner.	Being autistic doesn't mean I can't have a job/an education/ friends/a partner.	I think anyone's lucky to have (one of) those!	Why am I luckier than anyone else with a job/ an education/ friends/a partner?
Autistic/ disabled people are so inspirational/ exist to inspire the rest of us.	I like to inspire people through things I've done, but not just by existing.	I exist for the same reason as everyone else – whatever that is!	Do you think that's our only purpose?

I know how annoying it is when people are quick to patronise, or contradict, or make assumptions. Just remember, they are neurotypical and therefore lack autistic social skills, and we have the power to educate them!

CHAPTER 2

Overload

Too much information

One of the first things I remember about secondary school is trying to play football. I was surrounded by running, shouting kids who may or may not have been on my team, a ball that showed no mercy to any body parts it hit, and an angry teacher yelling at me for 'getting caught in possession'.

This is just one example of information overload. For different people, it may be a different situation. But whatever kind of situation you struggle with most, chances are it leads to that overpowering sense of turmoil that no words, actions, or even tears can fully express. I don't know about you, but personally, having someone shouting 'don't get caught in possession' several times does not help me in any way.

Even as an adult, I still cannot process complicated, ambiguous explanations/instructions, especially when there is a lot going on. A person will give them, and I will try to summarise what I think they are trying to communicate just to make sure I've understood, then what do they very often do? Paraphrase! Not even a yes or no to confirm whether or not I got it the first time. And my brain has to start all over again.

Because I struggle to distinguish between relevant and irrelevant information, I get confused when people bombard me with lots of detail or instructions. I need someone to give me a summary of the basics, preferably with the scope for me to ask for more detail if I want to. I also need people to be patient if I ask a question that I should already know the answer to. It might be that the information in question was given in a way that was confusing for me, or it might just be that I want to make sure I've understood correctly, or that it hasn't changed. I have faced many situations that would have been less uncomfortable if people understood this. And if I've been given a lot to think about, I need time to think. How has it affected me? What do I need to do next? If I get that time, it could delay others concerned. If not, I'll find it really hard to make a careful decision.

This makes some group interactions challenging. If I could, I would press pause and magically find someone who can help me follow what is going on. Most of the time, I can't keep up with who has said what and what I need to be latching onto. There is information coming from so many different angles (literally and figuratively). Neurotypicals have a tendency to go off on all kinds of tangents, randomly change plans, and talk all at once. I tend to find myself left out of group discussions unless I really concentrate hard on what is going on and how to join in.

Because of this, people have often thought of me as being shy. While I have always been prone to social anxiety, struggling with group conversations isn't always caused by shyness. My friend Abby has similar struggles to me in this respect:

> *"I struggle to hold a conversation with someone in a place where lots of people are talking because I can't filter out other conversations very easily. Just thinking about it gives me a headache. I have a bit of a reputation for being a quiet person in groups, but it's more about trying to concentrate and listen and then never knowing when to speak or chip in or even how to."*

If you know you are going to be dealing with a group situation that you are likely to find bewildering, try making a list of points about what you might find difficult. Even if you would rather tell people by mouth, it may be helpful to have a list for your own reference. My own example would be something like this:

- I retain information best when given in clear, step by step points by one person at a time. If too many extra details get thrown in, especially if it sounds like they contradict what you are trying to say, I will get confused.
- I learn new skills best when I do the task with someone talking me through it and by repetition until I have memorised what I need to do.
- I will struggle to keep up with a busy group conversation with lots of information being passed around, especially if emotion is high.
- I need any expectations as to what I'm supposed to do to be made clear to me on a one-to-one basis.
- I may sometimes ask a question that you expect me to already know the answer to. This may be because I wasn't aware, because I'm checking I've understood correctly or because I'm making sure nothing has changed.
- I cannot easily read non-verbal social cues such as facial

expressions and body language. This means I might not pick up on unspoken social rules and expectations as readily as most people.

- I find it hard to talk when there is something else taking up my concentration. If someone talks to me while I am concentrating on something, feeling overwhelmed, I may find it hard to respond.

And just remember…don't get caught in possession. Whatever that means.

Meltdowns and shutdowns

> *"[Meltdowns and shutdowns] are usually prompted by feeling socially overwhelmed. They often come from feeling trapped at an event, and I can't leave, […] or trapped by a difficult situation or task."* – Kathleen.

What Kathleen describes is a common struggle for people on the spectrum. When overwhelmed by sensory overload, social overload, too much sudden change, too many demands, or a combination of factors, many autistic people tend to experience meltdowns or shutdowns. The word 'meltdown' may be more familiar to most readers than the word 'shutdown', and they may be thought of as the same thing by some. Both are a result of an autistic person reaching crisis point and being unable to deal with their current situation, but they manifest in different ways. To put it briefly, a meltdown is an outburst of extreme behaviours such as shouting, crying, aggression, self-harm, and repetitive behaviours. A shutdown tends to be harder to spot and may present as withdrawal from the person's surroundings, reduced ability to communicate, and reduced ability to move away from the situation.[1]

Because big, emotional outbursts are not something I'm prone to, I tend to experience shutdowns rather than meltdowns. They don't usually come on suddenly. When I'm well outside my comfort zone, I will go into the mental equivalent of power saving mode. I keep my head down, remain on the sidelines, and withdraw into my own head.

If I have an obligation to be in this place, I will do what I think is expected, but though polite, will not be at my most sociable. Nor at my most attentive. My brain is doing only what it has to. As soon as it is socially acceptable, I will recharge in the seclusion of my own room and start to feel more human pretty quickly.

While in power saving mode, I may find it hard to talk. Not because I lose the ability to understand or remember words. Nor because there's anything wrong with my voice or mouth. My brain is just too busy to convert my thoughts into words. Talking requires concentration. It means thinking about what I should and shouldn't say. It means figuring out how to put the images and concepts that are in my head into words. It means talking in a tone that neurotypical people like. It means being on high alert for social cues that I'm not naturally good at noticing. Power saving mode means my brain needs to prioritise dealing with my situation, and I don't have the capacity for trying to figure out how neurotypical people expect me to act.

Now turn it up a notch. I'm in such a place for too long, or there are too many demands being made, or maybe I'm in a difficult situation with a person. At this point, even power saving mode is wearing thin. Until it becomes… shutdown mode. For me, that means feeling as if my brain and emotions have reached breaking point. I might suddenly have to leave the room because I can't take any more. I might cry because of some small trigger that unleashed festering negative feelings. I might be uncharacteristically irritable.

I might be desperate to shield my senses from the outside world but not know how. Most likely, I will be stuck in a daze with my mind in turmoil and my social skills gone. I will invariably be too stressed, bewildered, and unfocused to function. But because I mostly internalise and withdraw, I struggle to communicate what I need and how I'm feeling. I may just come across as flustered, stupid, even more socially awkward than usual, antisocial, or moody.

It is also common for autistic people of all ages to be able to manage a draining situation well enough while it lasts, but then go into power saving mode – or have a meltdown or shutdown – afterwards. Abby is a classic example of this:

> *"I have long periods of not speaking because I'm busy processing or calming – I can't come home from work or a social gathering or finish a phone call and immediately enter into another discussion or download anything about it. My family respect that we all shut away at times, and it's nothing personal."*

Similarly, I can remember coming home from college and John, my stepdad, asking me how my day was. I couldn't give much of an answer because I needed time for the events of the day to fall into place in my brain, away from noise and other people. He kept trying to get me to be more conversational when what I needed was to be away from any social pressure, and to talk about my day in my own time. But because I was so mentally depleted, I didn't have the capacity to figure out how to explain this.

There are different ways of dealing with meltdowns and shutdowns, and you may already have your own coping strategies in place. To manage future situations that you are likely to find overwhelming, it might help to write down what a meltdown or shutdown means for you and what might trigger one. This can be useful for showing to people for future reference and can help you understand yourself better too. When facing a high-stress environment – for me, it would be airports, very large train stations, or my graduation ceremony – plan when and where you could take a breather. Learn in advance what to expect from the occasion. Stick with someone who understands you well. And bring a book, or an iPod or phone, or anything else that helps you calm down.

Whichever coping methods you come up with, try to use them while power saving mode is still working. Because the more you are struggling, the harder it may be to communicate your needs. It's not easy telling others about what feels like a weakness, especially one that the majority won't have experienced to anything like the same extent. But the people around you have a right to know. And you know what? You have a right to not suffer in silence.

Autistic masking

We all spend a good chunk of our lives trying to present ourselves in a certain way to please other people. I think of it as being like putting on a mask. Relatable, right? You might wear an 'I'm fine' mask when you are feeling miserable. Or an 'ideal version of me' mask when with people you can't quite be open with. Or an 'I'm in control of my life' mask when you suddenly realise you are an adult.

Or a 'presenting as neurotypical' mask as an autistic person. Let me explain.

Masking is when someone on the spectrum consciously or unconsciously suppresses their natural autistic traits and learns how to display neurotypical ones in order to fit in. It is very often done out of fear of standing out or making a mistake. This is how Kathleen describes it:

> *"Social situations often feel like such a performance for me, even when with people I know and love. I feel the pressure to 'put on my personality'*

each day and sometimes even prepare a few funny anecdotes or things to talk about before meeting up with someone or going to an event. I wish this were something people talked about more."

The sad thing is, masking is still too easily encouraged, implicitly or explicitly, by a society that places so much importance on following neurotypical norms instead of accommodating and accepting differences. It can involve:

- Not stimming (i.e. not displaying repetitive behaviours that help you feel calmer, such as fidgeting, hand flapping, pacing, playing with hair, etc.).
- Forcing yourself to make eye contact and concentrating on how to do so in a neurotypical way.
- Trying not to react to uncomfortable sensory stimuli.
- Planning possible things to ask or talk about in a conversation.
- Copying neurotypical behaviours and body language.
- Pretending to understand what someone is talking about or what is going on in a situation.
- Trying to hide unusual interests, abilities, or weaknesses.

Now, these may sound like things that everyone has to do at some point in their lives. However, when you are outnumbered by people with a different neurotype, you may spend so much time masking that you don't know how to show your true colours and be yourself. Or you may burn out altogether.

This is something I can relate to all too well. With my mask, I can listen to someone without breaking eye contact to look at everything else around me. With it, I can laugh at my own mishaps without getting frustrated or embarrassed. I can stop myself reacting to people I don't know well touching me unexpectedly. I can go to parties and have fun while fighting the feeling of being both overcrowded and isolated. I might downplay my detailed long-term memory of past conversations or events or my extensive knowledge of anything 'nerdy', so people don't think I'm weird. I might hide how bad my short-term memory and awareness of current news and trends are, so people don't think I'm stupid. I can not only make small talk but also put new people at ease with my sense of humour. With my mask, I can manage rather a lot.

But when I'm struggling to keep it up, I say the bare minimum to people, especially new ones. When the mask slips, I get irrationally angry about any mistake I make, autism related or not. I am slower at understanding sarcasm and jokes and interpreting instructions. I either avoid social events or go and spend the whole time feeling desperately lonely and self-conscious when everyone else knows how to bond in a big group. I am very easily confused by too much background noise or too many people talking at once. When I'm in the middle of a shutdown, a panic attack, or feeling upset, it's like I've dropped the mask altogether, like in the picture. I can't face anyone other than – at most – my parents, and I may even find it hard to talk. Alternatively, if I'm with someone I feel safe around and I start talking about how I'm feeling, I may go on for ages without putting any mental filter on what I'm saying.

When I am managing a situation well, it may be something I am at ease with, but very often, I will simply be wearing a mask of social rules and mannerisms that don't come naturally, that I have spent my whole life trying to learn. When I am not managing well, it might be that I don't know how to deal with the situation I'm in, but it might also be that I don't have the energy for masking. I have experienced the latter many times. In those situations, I have often felt bad afterwards for not making more of an effort when I might have been able to communicate in the expected way if I had really pushed myself. In hindsight, however, I think I was burning out from all the effort I'd been putting into dealing with prior social situations without even realising it.

Meanwhile, well-meaning people have been surprised to see me shut down or burn out, having seen how easily I appear to pass as neurotypical in other situations. Often, they have tried to be encouraging and said things along the lines of 'you can do it' or 'you were doing so well before, you can keep going'. I realise words like these can be helpful when someone is anxious and seeking reassurance or when they are struggling to learn a new skill.

When I am feeling drained from socialising or masking, however, what I would like people to bear in mind is this: imagine you need to pick up and carry a very heavy box. If you are careful and know what you are doing, you can probably get it off the ground fairly easily. You can still talk while holding it. You can walk around. You may even be able to walk up or down a set of steps.

But then imagine you have to carry it on an hour-long walk without stopping and without putting it down. By the time an hour has passed, you have long since had to give up because you are exhausted. People might say things like 'but you were carrying it so well an hour ago. You can keep doing it!' Or worse, 'why are you so tired? We weren't walking that fast'. Or someone who didn't see how far you carried the box sees you being unable to walk with it now and thinks you are weak or incompetent.

Sometimes people find autistic behaviours weird or annoying when I am displaying them because I am unable to act in a more neurotypical way. Like when there is an argument (especially within my immediate family), people find it annoying when I have a shutdown, even though it's something I cannot help. Other times they look for some hidden reason or intention behind autistic behaviours – or things I say – when there isn't one. In these situations, the main reason is: I am not neurotypical, and I cannot always pretend that I am.

Anxiety and burnout

> *"I used to have two jobs to pay for rent and bills. [...] Sunday involved singing in the worship at church and leading the Sunday school. I didn't have time to make sense of my feelings or relationships. My role as a mum and thinking about getting in touch with family was more overwhelming with two jobs. Work took over, and I could not keep up. I had 4-5 hours of sleep a night. My GP wrote me a sick note, and I had two weeks off both jobs. All I could do was rest."* – Luna.

As Luna's experience shows, being autistic in a neurotypical world can be exhausting. Those of us on the spectrum put so much brainpower into making sense of it all that we are bound to burn out. It can be for any number of reasons: stress, too many social demands, over-empathising, and sensory overload are just a few. It can be a short-term reaction to having a hard time or a long-term reaction to ongoing unprocessed trauma. Very often, it is a result of repeated overwhelm. Some neurotypicals refer to burnout as autistic regression because signs of autism become more apparent, having been masked for too long. I don't like this term, as it implies that presenting as neurotypical is better and autistic is worse. Also, there aren't many resources out there that talk about burning out, and the ones I have found mainly address parents of autistic children. This makes it hard to know how best to write about it but all the more important to do so. Here are just a few ways in which burnout may present:

- Reduced ability to handle situations that you can usually manage.
- Increased difficulty with social skills.
- Inability to mask, either from forgetting how or simply not having the energy.
- Fatigue – can be physical, mental, emotional, or any combination.

- Unwanted physical symptoms, such as stomach aches, abdominal pain, shaking, and headaches.
- Heightened anxiety.
- Mental illnesses or a relapse of pre-existing mental illnesses.
- Panic attacks.
- Feeling like you're in an ongoing meltdown or shutdown.

Looking back, I have always been prone to anxiety and burning out. This was a particularly common problem at school, college, and university, and until recently, I didn't really develop any coping strategies other than waiting for it to pass. If I were at all able to get through a draining situation – short-term or long-term – I would until I just couldn't. I would constantly be trying to do whatever I thought was expected of me while feeling frustrated at having to put so much extra effort into making sense of people and their expectations. I often experienced physical symptoms, something I'm still prone to. Some days I had to go home with unexplained nausea. Some nights I took ages to get to sleep, only to wake up feeling sick, shaky, and anxious. Here are some excerpts of my mum's explanations of how anxiety and burnout presented in me:

> *"Grace [...] is spending so much time and energy on coping with her surroundings that after a few weeks into the school year, her energy and ability to focus decline. By the summer term, her reactions are very slow. She also suffers from stress headaches."* – report on evidence of my autism (April 2002).

> *"Constantly getting things wrong leads to isolation and intense frustration that Grace finds hard to express, so she gets depressed – goes off her food, suffers disturbed sleep patterns, increased distractedness, and reduced ability to function and cope. She gets very lethargic and withdrawn and obsessive and much more panicky over small things..."* – extract from my Disability Living Allowance application (November 2005).

> *"Grace at present gets quite frequent anxiety-related psychosomatic symptoms, most commonly 'feeling queasy', and hot and/or cold. She will often say that she is not worried about anything then later tell us about some interpersonal conflict or friend who is unhappy for some reason."* – comments for a review meeting (November 2006).

Later, when I was at university, I sometimes got migraines and would need to lie down in my bedroom with minimal noise and light and try to sleep through the pain. I didn't have any kind of illness as far as I could tell; it was all down to the ongoing stress of not knowing how to communicate in a way that people could understand or accept.

Over the past few years, I have felt like I have a higher capacity for socialising than I used to. More recently, I have come to realise that I can push myself harder and 'mask' for longer but still burn out if I'm not careful. I have had to learn to recognise when I have reached the stage where I am still able to carry on if I have to, but I am beginning to wear out. At this stage, I will be less able to enjoy things I would normally enjoy, with mental energy going down. I may be coping with the main source of my stress as best I can but unable to handle smaller things without having a shutdown.

In the lead up to Christmas 2019, when I was juggling work, present shopping, Christmas socials, and festive musical events, I had very little time to myself and was consequently exhausted. To get through it all, I deliberately set time aside for myself most days to be alone in my room and read, draw, colour, or journal, without worrying about upcoming events or things I still needed to do. This was because setting aside some quiet time *was* one of the things I needed to do. When I made sure to have one evening a week where I didn't cook, go to the gym, or go to any social events after work, it gave me enough of a boost in energy to keep being busy the rest of the time.

Anxiety has many different causes, similar to those that can cause meltdowns, shutdowns, and burnout. It can be due to work pressures, issues in personal relationships, e.g. conflict, recent trauma, bullying, political or worldly events, or unprocessed past trauma. These are common struggles for neurotypicals as well as autistic people. Those of us on the spectrum also have the added burden of feeling unable to be ourselves without being questioned, judged, rejected, or even abused. We may be desperate to prove ourselves and avoid making mistakes. Many of us have learned not to trust our own judgement. As a result of these struggles, I am still prone to overanalysing my mistakes in a social or work setting, feeling like a burden, and expecting to be rejected by others as soon as they experience my shortcomings. Is it any wonder why anxiety and mental illnesses are so common in people on the spectrum?

Sometimes, phases of prolonged and/or intense anxiety can lead to an anxiety attack or panic attack. Although an anxiety attack may present in a similar way to a shutdown on the outside, it feels like a different thing. During a shutdown, I will simply be tired, confused, frustrated, overloaded, and unable to function well. For me, an anxiety attack is characterised by intense fear that goes beyond the level of stress or worry one would expect to feel in their current situation, accompanied by physical symptoms such as nausea, vomiting (rare for me, but it has happened), abdominal pain, shivering, feeling hot and/or clammy, and rapid heartbeat. During an anxiety attack, I will be in shutdown mode, but when I have a shutdown, it doesn't necessarily lead to an anxiety attack. An anxiety attack is usually short-lived, but always horrible while it lasts.

Luna regularly struggles with anxiety and has learned a few tips on how to deal with it:

"I will go quiet while everything goes round in my mind. It is my [Christian] faith that gets me through anxiety. [...] I recently went on a wellbeing course. They told me to distract myself from thoughts by doing other activities such as walking, craft, cooking. Our minds think less on the anxieties and more on what we are doing in the present."

To follow on from Luna's advice, here are some pointers I have come up with on dealing with anxiety and burnout:

- **Try to make time for recharging *before*** you start to need it desperately.
- **Identify early signs of feeling burnt out**. For me, they are increased frequency of physical symptoms, difficulty sleeping, difficulty with social skills that I can normally manage, and a general sense of anxiety even when I'm not consciously worrying about anything specific.
- **Identify what helps you recharge**. For me, these are mainly creative pursuits such as reading, art, and journaling anything that is bothering me, but will mean something different for everybody depending on your talents and interests.
- **Identify what you find draining** – including things you have to do and things you enjoy doing when you have enough energy, like certain social events. Other examples could include sensory overload, any situation where miscommunication and misunderstanding are common or trying to do a lot of different things in a short space of time.
- **Try to reduce screen time before bed**. If I have all or most of a day to myself, I will happily treat myself to a film or an episode of something. However, if I only have an evening or part of an evening, I self-regulate more effectively if I am doing something relaxing that doesn't involve scrolling mindlessly through social media or YouTube.

- An anxiety coping mechanism I have developed: when anxiety is threatening to overwhelm me, I **repeat the lyrics to a calming song** in my head. It forces me to slow my thoughts down and focus on something soothing and familiar.
- When you have a lot on your mind, **try writing down all the things you are thinking about**, as it can give a sense of control over these thoughts. It also gives you a little more perspective in that you can see which things are bothering you the most and also which ones can be dealt with and when.
- I've often heard people say that **concentrating on breathing deeply and calmly helps**. A variant of this strategy that once got me through a panic attack is to slowly breathe in and then blow out. It's as if I'm channelling all my discomfort into the blowing until I've blown it all away. You might want to try blowing in a certain direction. If outdoors, you could aim for a cloud or anywhere in the sky. If indoors, maybe aim for a door, window, or light. I know you can't literally blow physical or emotional discomfort out of you, but I found it really took the focus away from how bad I was feeling.
- **Wind down before bed.** Take at least half an hour to do something that slows your thoughts down, like reading, drawing, colouring, listening to relaxing music, or even meditating.
- If you can't sleep, **get up and do something soothing.** Draw, colour, read a book. Then try again. For me, this turns a bad night into an ok night and means that I…
- …**don't spend the whole night feeling frustrated about being unable to sleep.** Frustration will keep you awake in a vicious cycle if you let it.

- **Try not to look at the time during the night** unless you are sure it's nearly time to get up. Doing this will only make you more stressed about how much more time you have to sleep.

And finally, one last thing to remember is that it's ok and normal to not be functioning at your best all the time. Thanks to having to work so hard to get by in a neurotypical society on top of the usual pressures of adult life, it's easy to forget that burning out is a part of being human. You might get burnt out from different things to other people or express it in a different way, but that's ok too.

It's also easy for the people around you to forget, and even when they have the best intentions when trying to get you to be sociable, it's ok to set your boundaries and explain to them that you are feeling overloaded and cannot deal with it right now. Some people may react negatively, and that's frustrating, but it's their problem, and it shouldn't stop you from taking care of yourself. Besides, there are many people out there who will understand and be sympathetic. Sometimes the only way to get back to functioning at your best is to accommodate the times when you need to recharge.

Explaining your needs to other people – points to consider and some examples

As with many autism-specific struggles, there will always be situations where neurotypicals might benefit from understanding what overload might mean for an autistic person. I've already mentioned how tricky it is to explain certain aspects of yourself to people who don't understand. When you are in the thick of a meltdown, shutdown, or burnout, you probably don't have enough mental energy left for putting it into words. If so, prepare to talk to someone about it in advance by considering the following points:

- **What do you find overwhelming?** E.g. Too much noise, too much light, too much social pressure, too much social interaction without a break, too much 'busyness', information overload.
- **How might you act?** E.g. Might zone out, cry, be less able to communicate, be more easily confused, seem angry or scared, self-harm, display repetitive behaviours to self-regulate, be less able to behave in a neurotypical way either due to forgetting how or not having the mental energy, be less able to handle tasks or decisions.
- **How does it feel for you?** E.g. Exhausting, embarrassing, frustrating, humiliating, scary, physically painful.
- **What helps you feel better?** E.g. Having a close friend or family member to talk to, sensory comfort, music, alone time, people understanding that you aren't being awkward or antisocial on purpose or because you don't care, being aware of what is going to happen, being updated regarding any changes, having a safe outlet for frustration or other strong emotions, clear and concise communication.
- **What doesn't help?** E.g. Impatience, jokes or sarcasm (even if you are usually good with these), people ignoring you or refusing to cooperate with you until you behave in a neurotypical way, certain sensory stimuli, information overload, being told to calm down (or anything along those lines).

And if, on the other hand, you are fully able to describe a meltdown, shutdown, or burnout while you are experiencing it… please tell me how you manage it!

CHAPTER 3

Friendship

Making friends

I used to spend years watching other people at school or college, wondering how they had such close-knit friendship groups, while I just didn't feel close to anyone. I hope the above picture does justice to that feeling! Even now, I will spend the best part of a social situation staying with someone I know or on my own like a hermit. Does that sound familiar?

Finding true friendship can be a real struggle for autistic people surrounded by neurotypicals who may not always know how to accommodate someone who's a little bit different. This is something that Abby has often found hard:

> *"There have been many situations where I've been hurt by thinking someone liked me or wanted to get close, but actually it was something else they wanted [...] I find that a lot of people seem to need a high level of ongoing interaction in order to feel like the friendship is being maintained [...] I don't need those high-intensity interactions as I feel stifled by them, so good friends are few."*

As an adult, I've been lucky to find more close friends than I ever managed while I was growing up. While no two friendships start off in the same way, in my experience, they have started due to shared experiences and similar interests. I've heard people say that if you never meet people, you'll never make friends. That is easy to say, but I find places full of people draining. If I am in such a place, it could be because I have to be or because I already know enough people for it to be enjoyable. And yet that is very often how I have ended up making new friends: by attending a social event where I already know someone well and so feel at ease enough to chat to other people.

One of the most common ways of making friends is bonding over something you both do together on a regular basis. You might start chatting to the same person, or the same few people, at college, university, or work. Or somewhere you volunteer. Or at a group that does something you enjoy. For me, that would be at a choir or in an orchestra, but I realise not everyone's hobbies are as nerdy as that.

It may help to pay attention to which people in these places you naturally spend more time with, and if they seem nice, maybe make an effort to talk about whatever it is you are doing in this place. It can be hard to know what to say to really connect with a new person. I find it can help to observe what sort of questions people ask you to try and get to know you and ask the same, or similar, questions yourself.

To complicate things further, true friendship is more than just making small talk. It may start off that way if you see someone a lot, but it requires more than simply being with them regularly. Keep finding things to talk about with them. If you are in a social group, you probably have an interest in common, so ask them about it. How long have they been playing that instrument or that sport? Is this just a hobby or an ambition? Give your opinions too, but don't forget to take it in turns to talk. Just remember: make them feel interesting and observe what you have in common.

Another thing to remember is what sort of things are appropriate to talk about with whom. There have been too many scenarios where I misjudged how open I should be with someone. I can remember the awkward moment of silence on my birthday years ago when I told my friends that it was on my fourth birthday that my mum officially found out my dad was cheating on her (true fact). I can remember accidentally ending a conversation about school experiences with someone I'd just met by talking in detail about the boys who tried to flirt with me while making racist remarks (sadly, another true fact). While most people struggled to get used to social distancing in 2020, it's something that I've been accidentally causing long before it was required!

Anyway, with that in mind, I have come up with a list of topics, and at which stage in getting to know someone it is appropriate to talk about these things.

A new person who you are just getting to know

- Where do they live (not their exact address, just the area)
- Your thoughts on the weather
- What do they like to do in their spare time
- What are they studying/doing for a job

- What do they like about what they are studying/doing for a job
- How do they know the person who introduced you to each other (if someone did)
- Do they have any pets
- What sort of things are they interested in

Someone who you have spoken to several times and get on well with

- Previous points if you haven't already broached them, plus…
- What are their thoughts on recent worldly events
- If they are engaged in paid or unpaid work, how is it going (though not everyone will want to think about work when not doing it, so be ready to move on to another topic)
- What are they doing/have they done over the weekend
- What are they passionate about at the moment

Someone who you talk to and spend time with on a regular basis

- Previous points, plus…
- How are their family members, pets
- What do they think and feel about whatever the setting is that you see each other in
- Continuing previous conversations to see how things have developed since the last time you spoke
- What little things in their life are proving tiresome or annoying for them at the moment

A close friend who is comfortable with discreetly talking about the following topics

- Personal struggles with family members, other friends, or a significant other
- Thoughts on politics
- Personal beliefs
- Money
- Embarrassing body-related details

When I did my internship at the Christian bookshop, the person who I worked with most was the assistant manager, who I'll call Marianne. She sat in on my interview, and when my soon-to-be boss had to leave the room, I awkwardly tried to make small talk with her. She didn't have much to say in return, and to be honest, I was relieved that I didn't seem to be under any pressure to be sociable with this person.

Once I got the job, Marianne played a large part in my training, and it was through working together that we got talking a bit more. Unlike the weekly discipleship course I was having to do that year, I was under no pressure to socialise and bond with lots of other people at once. I was given straightforward, methodical tasks to do, and when I wasn't doing them on my own, I was with someone else who liked to take her time to get to know people. Because we only talked when we needed to or when we felt like it, it was easier for me to relax around her and feel gradually more able to connect with her. Sometimes we would talk for ages (when we weren't serving customers). Sometimes we would work or sit together in silence. It wasn't long before one of us could warn the other with just one glance that we were dealing with a difficult customer and needed backup. The internship as a whole had its ups and downs, but it was largely my friendship with Marianne that helped me find the fun.

Some friendships happen when you least expect it. I met one of my closest friends, who I'll call Lizzie, at an orchestra we both went to nearly ten years ago. I had been playing my violin there for about a term when she first joined and was put in the seat next to me. When we got chatting, we realised we both had the same rather eccentric violin teacher and got into the habit of sharing violin lesson anecdotes. After a while, we bonded over our shared struggles with some of the music we had to play and our tendency to accidentally poke or nudge each other or knock the music flying. We sat together during coffee breaks and socials, and I really enjoyed her company and our jokes. When we realised we both love cats, that gave us something else to talk about. We started going out for lunch or dinner together. Lizzie was – and is – kind and funny, and I always look forward to spending time together.

When we went to university, I inwardly accepted we would be going our separate ways. Except we didn't. We messaged each other every few weeks and continued going to orchestra events and meeting up during the holidays. I was having increasing difficulties with maintaining healthy friendships and making new friends at this time, yet my bond with this one person was steady and uncomplicated. Gradually we came to rely on each other for more serious things. When Lizzie was having a hard time at university, I messaged her every week. Then some months later, she was the first friend I came out to about my sexuality (see Chapter 4) and played a big part in helping me accept myself and come out to other people. Now she is one of my most trusted friends. Who could have predicted?

Other friendships happen with the people you would least expect. Another friend of mine, who I'll call Joy, has an opposite personality to me in many ways. She is a spontaneous, fun-loving extrovert. I'm an introvert who thrives on alone time and careful planning. She loves social events and clothes shopping. I love reading, writing, and keeping to myself. We first met during our internship discipleship course (I was at the Christian bookshop, and she was the intern at her church). It took a while for us to get to know each other or even talk much one-to-one. For most of the year, we probably had the least interaction out of all the girls in the group. Then on a mission trip abroad that we all went on, Joy and I got talking a bit more and even found things to laugh about. Within a few weeks, we already had several inside jokes. Once the course was over, she was the only person I stayed in regular contact with.

These days, we understand each other and our differences pretty well and do a good job of balancing each other out. Joy helps me step out of my comfort zone while being aware that spontaneity and busy social events aren't my forte. I try to remind her to slow down and take a breather sometimes. We've been for walks, sleepovers, and shopping trips together. Over the years, we've accumulated a lot of inside jokes. We have our differences, but we know how to have fun together.

Stages/types of friendship

I should probably start by saying that the following paragraphs are only a simplified summary of how friendships can evolve. Very often, they will have elements of more than one stage. Having said that, knowing which of the following criteria most accurately describes your friendship with another person can be helpful in gauging where you stand with them.

The casual friendship

This is the person you may see on a regular basis who you get on well with and are used to talking to on a superficial level. You might even have a few jokes with them. You are comfortable enough with them, but you don't really confide in them about anything serious or go out of your way to be in touch when you don't see each other. Your friendship may evolve into a fun friendship or even a close friendship. It may also fade away when the two of you go your separate ways. Only time will tell.

The fun friendship

This is the friend who you are used to hanging out with away from wherever you naturally see each other. You may have at least one shared interest or hobby that you like to pursue together. You may have a lot of jokes together. You are used to doing stuff together because you enjoy each other's company, and you may even be able to confide in them to some extent when things aren't going well, though possibly not to the extent of the trusted friend. As with casual friendships, fun friendships could go in any direction. Very often, fun friendships are great while they last, but if they fizzle out, they tend to do so fairly quickly. On the other hand, when both friends grow to truly care about each other and learn to support each other when needed in the long term, a fun friendship can turn into a close friendship.

The close friendship

This is the friendship where both of you trust each other enough to turn to each other for support. Even if you don't see each other face to face for a long time, you still stay in touch a lot and maintain a close relationship. If you ever have any disagreements or even fall outs, you are able to resolve this in a healthy way without it having a negative impact on your friendship in the long run. You don't just have fun together; you also rely on each other. Close friendships can fizzle out or be broken, but it usually takes a lot for this to happen. Close friends usually only drift apart if something goes very wrong between them that they can't resolve or when they get out of the habit of contacting each other over a long period of time.

Empathy and listening

A few years ago, I found an article about a theory that some neurotypicals would consider ground-breaking: that autistic people do not lack empathy but instead are overwhelmed by it. I mean, I could have told them that, but I'm just glad that somebody did. Both neurotypical and autistic people struggle to understand each other, but because autistic people are in the minority, we are the ones who are thought to lack empathy.

Neurotypicals seem to rely heavily on cognitive empathy – that is, reading body language and facial expressions to understand feelings. Unfortunately, their reasoning often seems to be that because people on the spectrum cannot do this, we must lack empathy. There are several flaws to this logic. Firstly, taking longer to learn to read body language and facial expressions is not the same as being incapable of making sense of them until the day you die. Secondly, simply being able to recognise social cues is no substitute for knowing and caring about the person and their current situation. Although I struggle with superficial and practical communication, I have been able to pick up on others' emotions very acutely since before I can remember. This is called emotional empathy. When someone I care about is crying, I genuinely struggle not to cry with them. My friend Will is a classic example of this, as depicted in the following quote:

> *"When I feel someone else's pain, I feel it strongly. […] Many of us have too much affective and compassionate empathy, which can be overwhelming. Having empathy is what makes us who we are and what makes us more affectionate. I add empathy to affection. Everyone can do it; it's just everyone has their own way of showing affection."*

A while ago, someone asked me (not unreasonably): what are my thoughts on autistic people typically being logical thinkers, and how does it work being both autistic and emotionally sensitive? These days, my answer would be: speaking logically, when it's best not to, isn't the same as being unemotional. It's just that an autistic person may not realise they're being inappropriate. It doesn't mean we won't be upset if we offend someone. Trust me; my whole life, especially at secondary school, would have been a whole lot easier if this didn't bother me.

It took me a while to learn how to react to people's emotions, and I'm still learning now (not least because each scenario is different). As a teenager, I was completely at a loss for what to do when someone was upset, then hated myself for not helping. Now, I've honed my natural empathy so that I can get a sense of what a person needs from me, as well as how they feel. It gets easier once I'm in tune with how they think – having a similar personality, or knowing them a long time, helps.

In my experience, simple questions like 'do you need a hug?', 'Is there anything I can do to help?' or 'would you like me to do *x* for you?' can go a long way. Don't offer to do something you are unwilling or unable to do, and also remember to make it clear that you don't mind how they answer these questions. When you can learn to combine a cognitive understanding of the person's emotional needs and real concern for their wellbeing, congratulations – you have developed compassionate empathy!

One piece of advice I have often heard about listening to someone and showing them emotional support is to not talk too much about yourself and your struggles. This is one of those many social rules that applies more in some contexts than in others. When someone is having a hard time and turning to you for support, it's not helpful to make everything about you. It can make the other person feel like you're not listening, or that you don't care, or that you think you're more important. Sometimes, however, briefly talking about a time when you have struggled with something similar to what they're going through can help them open up to you and see you as someone they can relate to. It sounds confusing, and it may not always be easy to get the balance right, but I try to bear one thing in mind: am I keeping the focus on the other person?

Sharing my struggles – and having friends open up to me – has taught me a lot about the importance of empathy. It's more than sympathetic words and forced optimism. It's making it clear that you are there for the other person. It's remembering to check up on them when they are having a hard time. It's understanding that something may be a big deal to them even if it wouldn't be for you. Lastly, it's feeling their emotional burden and working out whether they're seeking advice, practical help, cheering up or – most likely – someone who listens and understands.

Listening dos and don'ts:

To summarise, here are a few pointers to remember when listening to a friend who needs your support. Some of them might sound obvious, but they are still important.

Do:

- **Keep the focus on the other person** while they are looking to you for support.
- **Listen to what they are saying** without interrupting.
- **Ask how they are feeling** about whatever they are talking about if this is not clear.
- **Let them know that they do not have to talk** about anything if they don't want to, but if they do want to, you are happy to listen.

- **Thank them for trusting you** if they have told you something really private.
- **Warn them if you think you need to tell someone else** about something they have told you in confidence (see below).

Don't:

- **Laugh** at them.
- **Be quick to judge them** or react negatively in any way.
- **Make assumptions** about whatever they are struggling with.
- **Tell them you know exactly how they feel** (you probably don't).
- **Turn the focus of attention onto you.**
- **Tell their secrets to anyone else** – unless they tell you something that makes you worry about their own or someone else's safety, e.g. suicidal thoughts, self-harm, bullying, harm to others, rape, sexual harassment, or thoughts of running away. Even then, only tell someone who you trust, and think can help.

Boundaries and conflict

> *"Be honest and be understanding of each other's boundaries. [...] set them fairly, and don't restrict the other person like some animal. Be truthful, with no deception and no lies [...]"* – Will.

Will makes a valid point here. Boundaries and conflict are uncomfortable but important parts of any human relationship. I am discussing them here because I have always found them hard and have been making a conscious effort to get to grips with them in recent years. From childhood until university, I used to think that the best way to maintain friendships was to let the other person have their own way all the time. I mean, that's what everyone says about friends; it's important to put the other person first. As a teenager, I was never good at interpreting social rules, and this one was no exception. It started harmlessly enough. If other children had forgotten/broken a pencil, they soon knew they could ask me for one. If we were queuing for anything exciting, I would willingly let anyone who asked to go in front of me. And if I had any particularly special treats in my lunch… well, you get the idea. I wanted to make people happy, and that was the only way I knew how. My first rule of thumb was to put other people first. My second was to avoid offending anyone. And saying 'no' to a reasonable request was, in my mind, the epitome of offence.

It wasn't until I started trying to apply boundaries that I learned that not having them makes it harder to recognise and respect other people's boundaries. At first glance, this makes no sense – the reason many people struggle to set them is that they desperately want to please. I've had to learn to not be either offended or overcome with guilt when people disagree with me or criticise me, and instead, work out how to change for the better. This doesn't mean blindly deferring to the other person. Sometimes it takes a bit of objective analysis of a situation to see what you could do differently.

Unfortunately, it's impossible to go through life without offending anyone. Until I left university, I used to think that being a good friend/family member meant keeping the peace at all costs, and that not doing so made me a bad friend/family member. It took me a while to realise that setting boundaries isn't unreasonable. In fact, it's important for working through problems in a healthy friendship. For me, it means:

- **Being consistent in the standards you set** for how you treat other people and how you expect to be treated.

- Not being afraid to politely but firmly **let someone know if you don't like the way they treat you.**
- **Being prepared to listen, apologise, and change your behaviour** where necessary when they don't like the way you treat them.
- **Being able to disagree with someone** while still showing them respect.
- Sometimes politely **reminding the other person that their way of seeing things isn't the only way** – while remembering this principle yourself.
- Being able to both politely **say no when someone asks you to do something you don't want or need to do** *and* not take it personally when *they* say no to something *you* ask.

Conflict has always been a major source of stress for me, especially when it happens within the family. I sometimes wonder if it's to do with early memories of family arguments, quickly followed by early memories of leaving behind everything I knew at the time. Having said that, according to my mum, I wasn't much better before then. My refusal to listen to any parts in *Pingu* storybooks in which characters got cross was a testament to that. My dear mother never tires of laughing at how often I insisted she change the word 'shouted' to 'said' when reading these books out loud. So clearly, my personality played a part.

And actually, it's hardly surprising that conflict can be hard for people with autism. Look at it this way; any social interaction requires the brain to be on high alert for the implication behind words and the very meaning of body language and facial expressions used. Now throw in some high emotions. Add a little anger (or a lot), some fear of making things worse, and a pinch of difficulty in expressing yourself eloquently. It sounds hard when you look at it like that, doesn't it?

We are often thought of as being logical and insensitive to people's feelings. For me, the opposite is true. On a good day, I like to think I'm pretty logical. I can analyse myself, other people, and most situations objectively. Unfortunately, I soak up people's negative emotions like a sponge. This can make any form of conflict overwhelming for me.

These days I'm aware that standing up for your needs isn't selfish or unthinkable because you can do so without tearing the other person down. Everyone deserves to be heard. And sometimes, you will do or say something wrong that hurts someone else, and it's important to be able to acknowledge it, apologise, and learn from it. My approach is to have some time away from the other person – not to guilt-trip them or sulk, but so we can both take a moment to calm down and process the situation. You may need to say to them that you need some time and space to cool down. Maybe do something that will help you feel better, like going for a walk, watching something relaxing, or engaging in a hobby or special interest.

Once your head feels a bit clearer, think about what went wrong, how you were hurt by it, and how you might have hurt the other person. Like me, you might find writing down your thoughts and feelings gives you a clearer perspective, as well as an idea of how to talk it through with the other person. Remember also to take a moment to think about the other person's side of the story. This can be a hard thing to do, but it is important to not get so stuck on your side that the conflict doesn't get resolved properly. Besides, if you can show them that you've thought about their point of view as well as your own, this communicates to them that you are mature enough to approach the situation fairly. At the same time, try not to get so overwhelmed by guilt that you are unable to learn from what happened and move on. A bit of guilt is important to help you learn from your mistakes. Too much can hinder it.

When you feel ready, try asking the other person – very politely – if they want to talk about what happened. If they say no, leave it a bit longer. You have to both be ready for it. Similarly, if they approach you first when you're not ready, it's ok to say you need a bit more time and space to process. When it's your turn to talk, rather than insulting them, expecting them to know how you feel, or saying things like 'You always…' or 'You never…', try saying 'When you said/did *x* I felt…'. And when it's their turn to talk, remember to listen and to try to understand. It might be worth asking them to explain clearly how they are feeling and what they want instead of expecting it to be obvious to you. Try to resist getting defensive, and instead try to listen and understand and apologise where necessary. When you can both talk it through, understand each other's feelings, and apologise, you will have come to a point where you can make up and move on.

Unhealthy friendships and how to get out of them

As with any kind of relationship with another person, friendships are not always straightforward. Chances are, you will go through good times and bad times with your friends. You will probably also have traits that annoy each other, as well as traits that you love about each other. No one is perfect, and everyone will make mistakes. This is normal.

But some friendships do not work out or can even be downright damaging for one or both people. This is a particularly common problem for autistic people. Understanding neurotypicals does not come naturally to us, and many neurotypicals' understanding of autism is even lower. And it's not always easy to know how to deal with toxic behaviour from other people. Kathleen has struggled with this, and the following quote from her shows how frustrating this can be:

> *"[...] At university, there was a particular person in my friendship group who didn't exactly bully me, but they made it very clear that they didn't like me and treated me very disrespectfully. It was really awkward, as we lived together and had a lot of friends in common, so there was no real way to avoid each other. Looking back, I really wish I stood up for myself more [...] I ended up ranting about this person behind their back, rather than calling them out on their behaviour."*

To complicate things, no friendship, just like no individual person, is all good or all bad. This can make it harder to tell the difference between a healthy friendship that simply has its ups and downs and an unhealthy – or toxic – friendship you need to leave. A mostly healthy friendship may have the occasional negativity, while an unhealthy friendship may still have certain positive aspects (which is what makes it hard for some people to realise it is unhealthy). It's important to look at the bigger picture here. If your relationship with another person largely fits the 'healthy' criteria, and any problems that crop up are addressed and overcome, you can be pretty sure you've got it right. To make it clearer, I have made a list of points on how to tell the difference.

Signs of a healthy friendship

- You don't always agree about things, but you still get along and respect each other.
- Mistakes and fall outs are infrequent, and you both know how to communicate your own side and listen to the other person's.
- Teasing is mild, and you both know when to stop.
- You both have other important relationships, but these don't get in the way of your friendship.

- You both have interests and hobbies that are outside of your friendship but don't get in the way of it.
- You support each other through problems.
- You can be honest with each other.
- You learn from each other.
- You are as nice when talking about each other as you are to each other's faces.
- You respect each other's boundaries.
- You are able to apologise to and forgive each other.
- Your friendship doesn't change even when you live far apart or go a long time without seeing each other.

Signs of an unhealthy friendship

- One person is dependent on the other.
- One person acts like a friend only when it suits them.
- One person repeatedly shows disrespectful behaviour.
- One person repeatedly makes the other person feel bad about themselves outside of what is considered a healthy boundary setting.
- One person takes the other for granted.
- One person tries to control the other.
- One person is jealous of the other.
- There is constant competition between you.
- One person lies, gossips, or can't keep a secret or promise.
- The friendship is mentally or emotionally exhausting for one or both people.
- The same problems keep happening with no improvement.

- One person continually refuses to listen when the other tries to explain their point of view after a conflict.

A few years ago, I had one friend who I was particularly close to. I'll call her Sandra. We stuck with each other at social events. We had a lot of shared friends and acquaintances. We did pretty much everything together. I still lacked confidence when it came to mixing with other people, but to me, that didn't matter because I was sure that this one friendship would last.

Sadly, this was not to be. My idea of being the ideal friend was to always put the other person first, no matter what. So when she made any decisions, I accepted them unquestioningly. When she wanted any changes made, I did my best to make them. The more I tried to be the ideal friend, the more I worried about making mistakes, which then irritated her. She started finding more and more small things to criticise me about, yet would be so sweet or good humoured when we talked about them that I couldn't find fault with her. If she were tired or stressed, she would be grumpy with me or only talk to me when necessary. If I showed concern or tried to help, this only annoyed her. I put up with all that because, after all, shouldn't friends put up with each other at their worst?

If I tentatively raised any issues I had with her, she would listen politely, explain her point of view, and voice any problems she had with me that I needed to change. I would feel so relieved at having talked things through; I would not realise until later that her word had been final and mine had been dismissed. She thought I needed to be less bossy yet described me as a pushover. She wanted me to give her more space but also to stop walking on eggshells around her. Meanwhile, I had no idea why I was so miserable at that time or so prone to physical anxiety symptoms. I frequently cried alone over a social faux pas I had made that she had pointed out or some deep-seated insecurity. I hated myself and my autism. I thought I was no good to anyone. All I knew was I wanted to be more like Sandra, and her approval would always make me feel better.

Things came to a head when what was meant to be a brief text exchange about where to meet before a social event turned into a massive argument about what had gone wrong between us. I felt like a failure and cried for ages. Yet this was the moment I realised I needed to make changes. I had become emotionally dependent on Sandra and her approval. I had neither understood her boundaries nor attempted to set my own. I didn't have the confidence to try to explain autistic communication styles to her because I didn't want to make excuses for myself. When she (reasonably or unreasonably) criticised anything I did, I felt so bad that I shied away from her like a kicked puppy instead of making sensible changes or explaining my perspective. I had often misjudged when I should talk to her and when I needed to give her space. I had been in a toxic friendship, and if I didn't make a stand for my own wellbeing, it could easily happen again.

The first step to getting out of an unhealthy friendship is realising you need to. The exact reason for needing to escape from an unhealthy friendship will be case-specific, but chances are, it has been a drain on your emotional resources, damaging your self-esteem, or holding you back in some way. Be clear with yourself about why this friendship isn't working. It'll be easier to be clear with the other person if you are clear with yourself first. Try writing down your thoughts and feelings to give yourself a sense of perspective. You will probably feel more able to remain firm in your decision if you can remember why you are doing this.

If your friendship is ending due to ongoing problems, as opposed to the two of you simply drifting apart, it is better to talk about it honestly and respectfully with the other person rather than avoid them without an explanation or do anything without telling them first. This may be hard, as you don't know how the other person is going to react, and chances are, you don't want to hurt them. As with smaller conflicts, the key is to be clear about why you are not happy with this friendship while not antagonising the other person unnecessarily. This means not being passive-aggressive with them, not insulting them, and not looking for revenge. Try to avoid accusing them and saying things like 'You always…' or 'You never…'. Instead, say 'When you do *x*, I feel…'. That way, you're not accusing them; you're just being honest about how you feel.

Remember, regardless of how well you handle the situation, how they react is out of your control. They may try to talk about ways in which they have been hurt by you. If they do so clearly and respectfully, try to listen to them and understand their point of view even if you are sure you are in the right. At the same time, do not let them push you around or manipulate you. Apologise if it is clear that you have done something wrong. Do not do so just to try and please them (this is something I know I'm guilty of). If they react badly, try to remain firm and respectful and re-emphasise what you have already said. If they keep refusing to listen, or if you cannot handle their behaviour, just tell them you have made yourself clear and that you are ending this conversation. And then do so!

If the other person is trying to end their friendship with you, that can hurt, and you may not know how to respond at first. If you don't feel able to handle it at that moment, tell them that you need some time and space to process it before discussing it. Similarly, if you need time and space to process it after the discussion, that is ok too. It's better to do that than explode in anger and do or say something you might regret. Listen to what they say, and accept that this friendship is ending, regardless of who is wrong in which way. Try to avoid begging or bargaining. You may find it hard to accept. You may feel sad, confused, or angry, and that's normal. But however you may be feeling, you can get through it without escalating the situation.

Dealing with a friendship break-up

I have often heard people say that a friendship break-up can be at least as painful as a romantic break-up. If you were on the receiving end – or even if you were the one who ended it – it's normal and understandable to feel a sense of loss. After my argument with Sandra, I tried to brush off my feelings as soon as I could and carry on with my life. Yet, I constantly found myself going over and over in my head what went wrong, what I wished had or hadn't happened, things that were said and done, and things that weren't that should have been.

I later realised that these feelings are a natural part of processing a loss. You need to let yourself feel sad. A friendship break-up *is* a loss, and you won't heal by forcing yourself to carry on as normal before you feel ready. This is a good time to immerse yourself in activities you find comforting, as long as they are not bad for you, and focus on other friendships, new and old.

You might also feel angry, or guilty, or both. This is normal, and it's important to be able to process these feelings. It is also ok to talk about how you are feeling to someone you trust, as long as you aren't going out of your way to make your ex-friend sound bad. Just don't let these feelings become destructive to you, the other person, or anyone else. If you can objectively see any mistakes you made, that's the first step towards learning from them. This isn't easy if you're angry with the other person for their mistakes or feeling so ashamed of yourself you are unable to learn anything.

You may also still have to interact with the other person sometimes, especially if you have a lot of shared friends and acquaintances. This may not be easy. When I fell out with Sandra, this had an impact on my interactions with people we both knew. Although I didn't fall out with anyone else, it soon became uncomfortably clear that quite a few of them were biased towards her. After asking me what had happened between us, some of them would point out where I had gone wrong with her, say they were sure things weren't as bad as I thought, or try to justify her behaviour. While they weren't necessarily wrong, it left me feeling increasingly alienated and that they weren't listening to my side of the story.

It took me a while to make new friends, and in that time, I had to learn to be on good terms with Sandra whenever we had to interact. At any social events we both attended, we gradually became more willing to make small talk with each other, however awkwardly. I like to think we managed to get through group interactions without making things uncomfortable for everyone else present. We learned to be friendly towards each other without getting too emotionally involved. By the time we properly went our separate ways, we weren't close, but we were on good enough terms. I still occasionally think about my past mistakes and hers, but I am at peace with both.

Seeing someone you have had a long-lasting fall out with can be difficult. Try to remain polite and respectful and don't bring up old issues with them. Nor should you say nasty things about them to other people. It will make you look bad, and they may well find out. It might help if, in a setting where you have to be around them, someone else is aware of the situation. Also, it's natural for mutual friends to want to stay friends with both of you. Don't try to force them to stop being friends with the other person. If their relationship with you hasn't changed, then don't worry about their relationship with your ex-friend. If, on the other hand, any mutual friends keep their distance from you, or are even hostile to you, then it's time to let them go as well. It can be difficult and sad when these things happen, but sooner or later, it will lead to better times with better people.

CHAPTER 4

Romance, Dating, and Sexuality

Before we go any further, I should probably get one thing straight: I am not. Straight, that is. I spent all of my teenage years and most of my 20s being afraid to acknowledge and accept my sexuality, and therefore afraid of finding love. This means that as I write this (aged 28, the year 2021), while I know about the highs and lows of love, I still haven't been in a relationship.

But romance and dating are a big part of life for most adults. So bear with me while I try to summarise my limited knowledge based on other people's input, my own observations, what I have read, and principles that apply to romantic and non-romantic relationships alike.

When and how to start dating

It's hard to know how to begin here because relationships can start at any time in adolescence and adulthood. Some people are quick to try dating while they are still at school. Others don't enter into a relationship until later in life. Some people meet the right person for them without even trying, while others might struggle to meet someone after weeks, months, or even years.

> *"My main thing to say on this topic is to be true to yourself. Don't aim to be in a relationship because it's the socially accepted thing to do. Examine whether it's something you actually want or whether you just feel socially pressured to date. You are whole as a person in your own right."*

Naomi's advice here is one thing I know from experience to be true. As an angsty, socially awkward adolescent, I used to long for a boyfriend. I wanted to fit in. I wanted to have something in common with my peers. I wanted someone my age to make me feel loved and accepted. But no matter how well I got on with boys or how hard I looked for attractive qualities in them, I just couldn't muster up any genuine interest in them. I didn't try dating them despite my lack of interest because it felt wrong to try to connect with someone so intimately when my heart wasn't in it. I know that some people do experiment with people of different genders to better understand themselves and their sexual preferences. Personally, though, I don't regret not dating people I didn't fancy at a time when I wasn't ready for a relationship anyway.

Regarding insecurities about falling behind other people, Kathleen shared with me a point made to her that I think is well worth holding onto:

> *"[...] My ex-boyfriend said something that really resonated with me. When I opened up to him about how I always felt I was behind everyone*

> *else in terms of relationships and sexuality, he responded with: 'Not by your own clock. By your own clock, you're right on time.'"*

This brings me onto my next point: how emotionally ready you are is more important than how old you are. I am feeling like a bit of a hypocrite for pointing this out when I can't help worrying about not finding love in my 20s. But relationships are a big deal, and if one person is not emotionally ready for one, both people will probably end up getting hurt. Here are just a few indicators of whether or not you are ready. You may also want to look out for these indicators in the other person.

You are ready if:

- **You are comfortable with being on your own** and not dependent on another person's company.
- You are not prepared to settle for **conditional love** – that is, love that depends on you meeting certain expectations.
- **You are happy** with where you are in life.
- **You have plenty of things and people in your life** that make you happy that are not related to dating.
- **You can accept that anyone you date will have flaws.**
- You are able to both **set your own boundaries** and **respect other people's.**
- **You know what traits you don't want** in a partner.
- **You are not afraid to be open and vulnerable** with another person.

You are not ready if:

- You want to be in a relationship **because everyone else is.**

- You are looking for a relationship **because someone else thinks you should be.**
- **You are struggling to move on** from someone you have loved before.
- **You are looking for someone to fix you.**
- **You are looking to fix someone.**
- **You just want sex.**
- **You are uncomfortable with the possibility of staying with the same person** for a long time.
- **You instinctively withdraw from people** when you get too emotionally close to them.

There are also many different ways of meeting someone. Some people meet online. Some meet at social events, including ones designed for people hoping to get a date. Some people get set up with someone by a friend. Some end up dating someone they've known for ages.

Thomas has some good tips on getting into the world of dating. His advice has been enlightening for me, not only in the context of this book but in thinking about my own life. His summary of the basics is as follows:

> *"[..] developing confidence and working on personal development is the best way to become more attractive. Work out, eat well, groom yourself, invest in some perfume or cologne. Hang around people with similar interests, as there's more chance you can get a conversation started about that interest. Clubs, themed meet-ups, and online dating can be a great path to finding those people – although be cautious when online; you don't want to be cat-fished [or] harassed."*

As well as listening to Thomas' advice, I have done a lot of research on how to increase your chances of meeting someone. I have also talked about different ways of dating with friends and family who are experienced in this area. The main pointers that most people suggest are as follows:

- If you feel comfortable with this, **let your friends and family know you would like to start dating.** They may be able to introduce you to someone.
- **Join a class or social group** that is relevant to your interests to increase your chances of meeting like-minded people. This also has the advantage of giving you and another person something to do together, as it can be awkward having only each other and your attempts at conversation to focus on!
- **Try online dating.** Bear in mind how widely online dating sites vary. Some are for people looking for hook-ups, while others are for people looking for a serious relationship. Some are exclusively for people of a particular sexual orientation or gender identity, while others are for anyone. Some may be for people from a certain culture or religion. Some may be for people within a particular age range.

Most people find the prospect of asking someone out terrifying. It doesn't have to be formal, however. It can be as simple as asking if they would like to meet up for a drink or a meal with you or if they would like to join you for a particular activity or outing. Make sure that wherever you go for your date is somewhere where both you and the other person will feel comfortable. You don't want either of you to be bored or uncomfortable, and you certainly don't want to try dating in a place that might trigger a meltdown or shutdown. Many people find in the early stages that it is easier to go on a date where you have something to do together. As with when you are looking for someone to date, you may feel more at ease if there is more to focus on than finding things to talk about. You will probably find that the activity in itself is a good conversation starter.

Unfortunately, finding someone to date and somewhere to go on a date is only the beginning. It seems like dating has all the harder aspects of making friends, but with much higher stakes! When you meet someone, you have to be able to gauge how interested they are in you and how happy you think you would be with them in the long run. You need to find things to talk about and do together. If you can keep the other person's interest and attention without being dishonest, then that is a good start. You may have to be on high alert for social cues such as body language and tone of voice. Here are a few examples of how neurotypicals express emotions through body language:

Social cues to look out for:

<table>
<tr>
<td>Attraction
• Smiling
• Trying to stay near the other person a lot
• Prolonged eye contact
• Standing taller and straighter
• Pulling in the stomach
• Flicking hair (mainly women)
• Mirroring the other person's posture and body language
• Looking at the other person's mouth
• Asking the other person a lot of questions about themselves
• Openly talking about themselves</td>
<td>Discomfort/ embarrassment
• Looking away a lot
• Looking at the floor
• Blushing
• Covering mouth
• Fidgeting
• Shifting feet
• Covering face with one or both hands
• Trying to change the subject in a conversation</td>
</tr>
<tr>
<td>Confidence
• Longer eye contact than most people
• Fingers closed
• Hands below chin level
• Upright posture
• Open arms</td>
<td>Anxiety/fear
• Biting lip
• Tense breathing
• Wringing hands
• Frequent swallowing
• Feet are pointing away
• Fidgeting
• Furrowed brow
• Tense shoulders</td>
</tr>
</table>

<table>
<tr>
<td>

Excitement/happiness

- Eyes wider but creased at the outer corners (think of this as an eye smile)
- Smiling with their mouth and their eyes
- Upright posture
- Frequent eye contact
- Talking animatedly

</td>
<td>

Impatience

- Tapping foot
- Drumming fingers
- Looking at the time
- Looking at the door or any other way out
- Hand on hip (one or both sides)
- Feet are pointing away (if standing)
- Crossing arms

</td>
</tr>
<tr>
<td>

Interest/listening

- Leaning forward while the other person is talking
- Frequent eye contact
- Occasionally nodding slowly while the other person is talking
- Tilting head

</td>
<td>

Boredom

- Yawning
- Resting chin on hand if sitting
- Looking away
- Fidgeting
- Slouching

</td>
</tr>
</table>

As with making new friends, getting to know someone on a potentially romantic level will take a fair bit of interaction. If you are nervous, it is ok to say so. You may find that it reduces the tension. I've been told that my guidelines for talking to a potential new friend can, to some extent, apply to conversations you have on a date (see Chapter 3). The thing to remember is that you are trying to connect emotionally. You are not just learning about the other person's name, occupation, hobbies, etc.; you are trying to get a feel for their personality and values. Ask them what they really care about or what makes them happy. Ask them about their achievements and ambitions. Exchange entertaining life anecdotes. By talking about these things, you are actively showing an interest in the other person and encouraging them to open up to you.

You may also be wondering if, when, and how you should tell the other person you are autistic, especially if they are not autistic themselves. This is another situation where some of the pointers from Chapter 1 apply. It is probably worth explaining what autism means for you during social interaction and that things like lack of eye contact, power saving mode, etc., do not mean you are not interested. If the other person is autistic themselves, your experiences as autistic people may be a great thing to bond over! Talking about autism to someone you are hoping to date may be especially daunting, but if you do not mention it until you are well and truly entering into a relationship, they may feel hurt by you not telling them sooner.

Finally, to maintain any connection made on a first date, people often find it helpful to stay in touch with the other person in between seeing them face-to-face. While messaging them constantly may annoy them or make them uncomfortable, doing so every few days can be easier and more comfortable than talking in person, as long as you both want to. You can take your time to figure out what to say and say it in your own time. Because of this, it can be easier for both sides to show their true colours without feeling under pressure to present themselves in a certain way.

Making a relationship work

> *"Relationships are hard. Everyone has their own flaws that we do and don't notice, so in that sense, you should view each 'attempt' as a learning process. You can't expect to get everything right the first time, especially if you struggle with social aspects or you throw everything on the line for that one person. There are numerous articles, videos and information online about relationships, the stages of them and the common difficulties. I even have a few videos for people in neurodiverse/ neurotypical relationships myself!"*

In the previous quote, Thomas has summed up the main message of this section: making a relationship work requires more than simply loving the other person. Once the novelty of the relationship has worn off, difficulties and conflict will arise. No two couples will have the same experience because everyone has different emotional needs and ways of expressing them, but there are some habits that most couples try to stick to in order to maintain a healthy relationship.

First, there is communication. This can be tricky in any human relationship and can be especially so for an autistic person and a neurotypical person as a couple. For neurotypicals, unspoken communication – body language, facial expressions, inference, etc. – seem to be instinctive. They expect us to not only pick up on these things but use them ourselves too. Then when we don't, we are left baffled as to what went wrong. If you are dating another autistic person, this may be easier, but you will still have your differences.

Whether your partner is neurotypical or not, it's important for both people to be aware of the differences in their communication styles and their reactions to different situations and to have conversations about this. How do you both express and deal with different emotions? What do you both need when you are experiencing these emotions? What makes you both feel loved? If unspoken communication is difficult for you, tell the other person this. For me, there are few things more frustrating than when people either expect me to know what they want without telling me or find a hidden meaning in what I say when there wasn't one. Explain to them how best to communicate with you, and be sure to ask them how they prefer you to communicate with them. If sometimes you need time and space to process and understand your own emotions, be clear about this before such an occurrence happens, and let them know that this does not necessarily mean they have done something wrong.[2, 3]

Being autistic may even give you an advantage here. Autism may sometimes add complications to a relationship, but given how open, honest, and dedicated many of us are, it can also be a real asset. We are less likely than neurotypicals to say or do things with any hidden meaning or motive. Once we are clear on what we need to say to someone, we have a knack for saying it candidly and openly. If the person you are with is receptive to this – or even better, communicates in a similar way – then that is a good sign.

On a similar note, it is important to be able to communicate positive things, as well as practical or negative things. Remember what it is you love, appreciate, and admire about the other person, be proud of their achievements, and tell them these things! To get a feel for how often, try paying attention to how often they express appreciation or admiration towards you. If they don't do this as often as you'd like, it may be that they are not aware of how big an achievement, or act of love, something is for you, in which case, you may need to explain to them. One thing to be aware of is that everyone has different ways of expressing love and affection. Some people find it easier to say it. Others find it easier to show it. Naomi and Kathleen both explain this well:

> *"[...] all autistic people express love differently. My sister and I are both autistic. She is very affectionate physically and with words. I, on the other hand, struggle to tell someone I love them [...] I'm more likely to show someone in making time for them and little gestures. [...] Partners need to take the time to understand both how the other person expresses love and what makes the other person feel loved and meet somewhere in the middle."* – Naomi.

> *"I suppose autistic people may show love through actions rather than words. Personally, I like to think of myself as a very loyal person. I'll go out of my way to remember specific things about the other person's life etc. – which I worry can come across as a bit creepy! I sometimes feel upset if the other person doesn't reciprocate in the same way or remember things about me."* – Kathleen.

Another big part of a relationship is physical intimacy. For most couples, this will largely comprise / consist of sex but will also include things like kissing, cuddling, holding hands, and other forms of physical intimacy. I am including this not just because of its significance in a relationship but because over and under sensitivity to touch are common in autistic people. As uncomfortable as it might be to bring up, this is an important thing to talk about with someone you are getting romantically involved with. In short:

- **What kind of physical contact do you both like or dislike?** If there are certain types of physical contact one of you doesn't like, or isn't ready for yet, the other needs to know.
- **When and where is the best time and place for certain forms of physical intimacy?** If, for example, one person likes to hold hands, hug, or kiss in public but the other doesn't, the first person may think the second isn't interested. Meanwhile, the second person may feel embarrassed by how often the first tries to initiate affection in front of other people.
- **How do you both express when you do or don't want physical intimacy in some form (including sex)?** If one person wants it but is communicating in a way that the other person doesn't understand, then they may feel like the other person is ignoring their emotional needs. If, on the other hand, they don't want it, but the other person isn't picking up on this, it will feel like the other person is ignoring their boundaries.

And finally, try to have fun sometimes! Try new activities together or indulge in your old favourites and make them into a tradition. Set regular time aside for dates and nights in. Arrange holidays and days out that you are sure you will both enjoy. Getting into regular habits and rituals will establish a sense of security, while new experiences will help keep your relationship feeling fresh and exciting.

Inappropriate behaviour and unhealthy relationships

Like many people, Luna has learned some hard lessons about relationships that go wrong. She has also learned the importance of both people feeling safe with each other, and I would seriously recommend taking the last sentence in the following quote to heart:

> *"I am not good with [dating and relationships] as I have had a lot of bad experiences. It is important to make sure your partner loves you above anybody else apart from Jesus. You need to be valued and respected."* (Note: this person has a strong Christian faith.)

As with friendships, not all relationships work out, and some can be downright toxic. I have been warned that autistic people can be particularly vulnerable to unwanted advances and toxic relationships with neurotypicals. We take people and the things they say at face value. We lack confidence in our own judgement. We have a strong need to get things right. Because of this, we can be easy to manipulate or take advantage of. We can also display toxic behaviour ourselves without realising. Relationships are never perfect, but if any of the below issues occur, take it as a warning sign that things need to change:

- One person makes hurtful comments about the other's physical appearance (this is called body shaming).
- One person feels entitled to another person's time, attention, or body and will not take 'no' for an answer.
- One person touches the other in a way that the other person doesn't like or feel ready for.

- One person only sees the other as a sexual being.
- One person gets in the way of the other person's non-romantic relationships and/or other parts of their life.
- One person tries to control, intimidate, or dominate the other.
- One person refuses to be clear about what they want from the relationship.
- One person is getting hurt by the other or is afraid of getting hurt by the other.
- One person is overly dependent on the other.
- One person shows no concern for the other's wants, needs, feelings and opinions.
- One person wrongly blames the other person's emotional struggles on them or an outside source or tries to deny the other's perception of events (this is called gaslighting).
- One or both are set on trying to form and maintain a perfect relationship instead of accepting that they both have flaws and trying to work through them.
- If two people are in what is supposed to be an exclusive, committed relationship and one or both have any sexual or romantic interaction with someone else.

Break-ups and rejection

The sad truth is that not all relationships – or attempts at starting a relationship – will be successful. When you start dating, there is always the chance that the other person will not be interested in starting a long-term relationship with you or vice versa. And even if you do get into a serious relationship, there's no guarantee that it will last. Unfortunately, this isn't something that you can compromise on, as you have to both want to be in a relationship in order for it to work.

When someone doesn't want to date you or decides they don't want to continue dating you, it can be hard not to take this personally. The other person probably isn't turning you down to hurt you. They simply do not feel able to be in a relationship with you, or maybe with anyone at the moment. You can ask them why, but only do so if you are prepared to listen to their answer or accept the possibility that they might not feel like answering.

If you like or love this person, then you will probably feel disappointed, sad, hurt, or even angry that they don't feel the same way, or that any feelings they had for you have died away. This is something I do understand, and I know from experience that you won't feel better overnight. As Thomas puts it:

> *"Break-ups are tough, and you will likely experience an intense, simultaneous feeling of longing and hatred. [...] The person you loved has changed into a life-destroying monster in your eyes. [...] Expect to feel horrible and find solace in time. If you don't feel awful after it ends, it's a good sign that there wasn't much there in the first place."*

You will need to take some time and space to heal from those feelings and let them come and go in their own time. Look for support in trusted friends and family members who will listen without judgment or putting pressure on you to mask. Engage in activities that are good for your body and mind. Try not to take it out on the other person, however. This does not make them a bad person, nor does it mean that you will never find anyone else. Be polite and respectful towards them and wait until you feel a bit calmer before trying dating again.

You may also find yourself struggling with guilt and self-loathing. This is a natural reaction to any form of rejection, especially when you have spent your life being made to feel as though you will never be as socially skilled as other people. Abby explains this better than I can:

> *"Break-up and rejection are hard [...] The way I try to look at it now is that relationships are two-way and break down because there's something that's broken the connection between you, not that there is something broken with one or other of you as such."*

In other words, unless the other person has said otherwise, you probably haven't done anything wrong. Something wasn't working between you, and you would not have stayed happy if you had stayed together.

Sometimes you may find yourself in the reverse situation, where you are not interested in someone who has asked you out or who you have already started dating. Or maybe you feel the relationship isn't working for you. Turning someone down can be hard because you don't want to hurt them, but if you are not attracted to this person or do not think you could be happy with them in the long term, it will be better for both of you. Be honest with them but be respectful too. Instead of making it sound like you blame them, just explain how you feel – you're not into them; you don't feel ready for a serious relationship, you do not feel as if it is working between the two of you. Do not waver and give in out of guilt or pity; if you do not want to be in a relationship with this person, you need to stand firm in this decision. How they react is beyond your control, but try and remain calm and respectful, even if they get upset or angry. Once you have explained your perspective, you have no obligation to keep interacting with them. If they turn threatening or won't take no for an answer, walk away from them. No matter what went wrong between you, they should not make you afraid for your own safety. Move into a public space, and if possible, meet up with or contact a friend or family member.

Coming out LGBTQA (+)

People have very different experiences of love, sexuality, and romance, and that's normal. Some people have had feelings for a lot of people. Others haven't. Some have dated a lot. Others haven't. Some have had a lot of sex. Others haven't.

There are also people who don't fit typical gender expectations, and that's normal too. Some men like fashion, animals, or the colour pink. Some women like sports, practical work, or technology. Many people don't strongly identify with either masculine or feminine stereotypes. I know I don't in many ways!

But while there are some people who simply don't follow gender conventions or who aren't in a rush to settle down with someone of the opposite sex, there are others for whom sexuality and/or gender identity are a real source of confusion and anxiety. My university mentor Laurie is well familiar with the intersectionality between the autistic community and the LGBTQA (+) community and has shared their own experiences with me surrounding autism, sexuality, and gender identity:

> *"There's a lot of evidence to show that gender and sexual identity presents differently in the autistic community. A disproportionately high number of us are transgender, non-binary, or gay. Most of the gay people and nearly all of the trans people I know are also autistic. I'm closer in kind to female on an autistic and emotional level but fall more heavily into male on everything else, including parenting."*

I am writing about this topic not just because it is a big part of my life but because autistic people are thought to be more likely to fall under the LGBTQA (+) umbrella than neurotypicals, as Laurie says. There are many different words relating to sexual orientation and gender identity. I have listed and defined some below:

- LGBTQA (+) – Lesbian Gay Bisexual Transgender Queer/ Questioning Asexual. The + sign refers to the many other sexualities and gender identities there are out there, but to keep things short and simple, I will stick with LGBTQA (+).
- Heterosexual (straight) – exclusively attracted to members of the opposite sex.
- Homosexual (gay/lesbian) – exclusively attracted to members of the same sex. The word 'lesbian' specifically refers to homosexual women. The word 'gay' is more commonly used to mean homosexual men but has been used more and more by lesbians (including myself – if I talk about gay people, assume that includes lesbians unless I specify otherwise).
- Bisexual – attracted to two sexes.
- Pansexual – attracted to people of any sex or gender identity.
- Asexual – not sexually attracted to anyone. Sometimes called 'ace' for short.
- Aromantic – not romantically attracted to anyone. Sometimes called 'aro' for short.
- Demisexual – can only be sexually attracted to someone they are already bonded to.
- Demiromantic – can only be romantically attracted to someone they are already bonded to.
- Greysexual/greyasexual – only experiences sexual attraction rarely and/or mildly. Sometimes called 'grey-ace' for short.
- Greyromantic/greyaromantic – only experiences romantic attraction rarely and/or mildly. Sometimes called 'grey-aro' for short.
- Cisgender – where a person's gender identity matches their physical sex.

- Transgender – where a person's gender identity doesn't match their physical sex.
- Non-binary – where a person's gender identity falls outside of the male-female binary, including the following:
  - Genderfluid – where a person's gender identity changes over time.
  - Genderflux – where the intensity of someone's gender identity varies.
  - Bigender – where a person identifies as two genders.
  - Trigender – where a person identifies as three genders.
  - Pangender – where a person identifies as any gender.
  - Agender – where a person doesn't have a gender identity or identifies as gender-neutral/non-conforming.

If you are autistic as well, being LGBTQA (+) can feel like yet another thing that singles you out as 'different' and makes you vulnerable to other people's ignorance and prejudice. I am writing about this because struggling to accept your sexuality or gender identity can massively impact one's experiences with love and dating. I still haven't had a relationship with a woman because doing so would mean acknowledging my sexuality, something that I have only just become brave enough to do. I'm less afraid of other people's opinions than I was, but I still feel it to some extent. Whilst I started openly talking and writing about being autistic in my mid to late teens and began to truly accept it after university, my sexuality remained a sensitive subject for me for many years. By the time you are reading this, hopefully, it will have become less of an issue for me.

I struggled to accept my sexuality for two reasons. One: I didn't want to be any more different than I already was. I was barely keeping my head above water socially and academically at school, I was filled with shame about how I just couldn't be neurotypical, and I couldn't face being in yet another marginalised category. Two: as I transitioned into adulthood, my social circle largely comprised Christians who were firm about gay people having to remain single. Some were very openly homophobic. I tried as hard as I could to get through the days when shame, and fear of what they would think, threatened to crush me. I also pushed down any feelings and desires I had about relationships and told myself that these weren't important and that I didn't need a partner. I kept going like this because, for the first time in my life, I had found a group of friends who understood and accepted me as an autistic person, and I couldn't bring myself to spoil it. I sometimes wonder if these things have stunted my emotional development when it comes to romance and sexuality in some way. I have only started processing them in recent years but have safely come out of the closet to my friends and family, who have all been extremely supportive.

Coming out requires courage. Believe me when I say I still haven't completely overcome my fear of it. It can be scary, awkward, embarrassing, emotional, and in a homophobic or transphobic community, even risky. It can also be liberating, cathartic, empowering, and something that secures a bond of trust – the trust you have in another person to feel safe coming out to them, and the trustworthiness on their part to be that safe person. It will make it easier to meet people like you, and it also increases your chances of finding someone to date. So how do you do it?

If you are going to come out to your immediate family, decide whether you want to talk to them all together or one at a time. I chose to tell my mum, stepdad, and sister at the same time over dinner. Telling them all together means you only need to do it once, while telling them individually may feel safer and more discreet, especially if some members are likely to be more accepting than others. Either way, your coming out journey is yours to make, and it is not for anyone else to either rush or hinder.

It also helps to be clear beforehand about what you want to say, especially if you are likely to be nervous or emotional. Write down a list of points if it helps you to prepare.

Example:

- I don't want this to be a big deal.
- I think you have a right to know.
- Feel free to ask questions/I don't feel ready to answer questions right now/While you can ask me questions, I may not always feel comfortable answering.
- It hurts me when people say *x* about LGBTQA (+) people.
- I've been planning on talking about this for a while.
- At the moment, I feel *x* about my sexuality/gender identity.
- Would you mind not telling anyone for now?
- I know what you believe about being LGBTQA (+) and your/our religion. I'm not trying to make you change your beliefs. I just want to know that you still care about me.

Despite what I might have made it sound like, it doesn't always have to be super serious. While I was still figuring out how to come out to Lizzie (who, by the way, has been amazing throughout my whole coming out journey), I messaged a university course mate, who I knew was bisexual, to ask for advice on coming out to a friend. Their suggestions were: a) say 'you know what's gay? Me!', b) make them a cake that says 'I'm gay' on it, or c) come out via a game of Hangman. I don't know what I had expected them to say, but none of that was it. Ultimately, I didn't follow any of the above tips, but hey, one of them might work for you! Lizzie, meanwhile, was incredibly sweet and understanding when I told her, and it was her ongoing support that helped me feel braver about coming out to more people.

These days, there are plenty of social groups and forums for people in the LGBTQA (+) community. If you are not fully open about your sexuality or gender identity, getting involved with them may feel like a big step but will probably really help you to feel comfortable thinking and talking about it. You will have found a reliable source of advice, you may make some valuable friends, and you may even get lucky and find love!

If you think that coming out to anyone you live with will put you in danger, e.g., violence or homelessness, it may well not be worth the risk. If you have any friends or family members outside the home who you could tell, come out to them and ask them for support. If not, look up a support group online. Whatever your circumstances, try to surround yourself with people who are accepting. This is easier said than done. It won't always be realistically possible to cut people out of your life, but you can move towards only letting new people into your life who accept you and being open about your sexuality/gender identity from the start.

Awkward and negative reactions to coming out

When you disclose your sexuality or gender identity, some people may make assumptions or ask inappropriate questions. I realise that this probably isn't what you were hoping to hear! If it is any reassurance, people responded far more positively than I dared hope when I came out. But I need to acknowledge that there is always a slight risk of hostility, especially from people with anti-LGBTQA (+) religious beliefs or from those who simply don't understand. They may think you are pushing the LGBTQA (+) agenda in their face. Please be assured that you are not doing so by simply talking about your struggles and that LGBTQA (+) people have to put up with far more heterosexual/cisgender agenda than vice versa. Some may even think you are doing it for attention. There is nothing attention-seeking about coming out. You are being real, open, and honest, and you have every right to say as much.

Also, despite all the evidence to the contrary, there are people who think that you cannot be autistic and LGBTQA (+), or that autistic people who think they are LGBTQA (+) are just confused. To put it bluntly, this is a load of bull! Being autistic does not mean you are incapable of understanding yourself or that you shouldn't be taken seriously. Even if you are not 100% certain of your orientation or gender identity, hold onto the fact that you know more about it than they do!

Then there are people who ask you overly personal questions. These may range from questions about your relationship history to your sex life or even your genitals! When faced with a situation like this, you can answer honestly and concisely. For example, if someone thinks you are wrong or confused about your sexuality because of who you have or haven't dated or had sex with, you can say 'I don't have to have had experience with [people of whatever gender] to know that I want it/don't want it'. Or 'My relationship decisions are not always connected to my personal feelings'. You can also choose not to answer at all, in which case, you can say 'I don't feel comfortable talking about this' and leave it at that. You have every right to correct any false assumptions, but you have no obligation to.

When faced with uncomfortable/negative reactions or questions, it can be hard to know what to say. This may be especially true for autistic people, when we may also be trying to communicate in a neurotypical friendly way or trying not to have a shutdown or meltdown. One thing to remember, as I have mentioned previously, is that if a reaction, statement, or question is uncomfortable, it doesn't necessarily mean that you should cut that person out of your life. Everyone makes mistakes, and if someone you tell ultimately accepts you and is genuinely trying to understand you, that is what matters.

CHAPTER 5

College and University

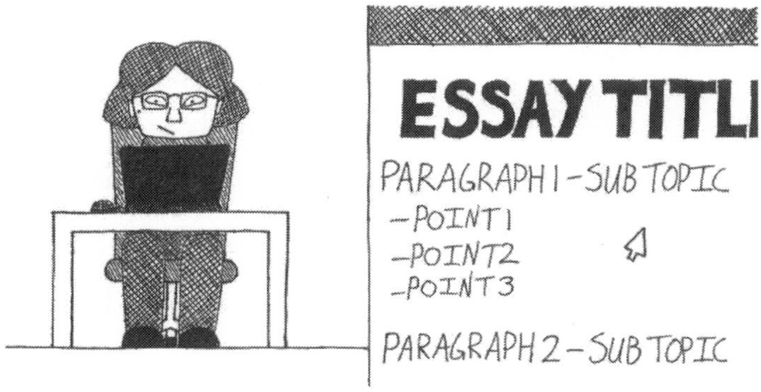

The social scene

I've often heard people say that further and higher education – if you pursue it – will be an important time in your life. You go there to study the skills and knowledge you need in your chosen career path. You may meet some long-lasting friends there. You will probably get a taste of the highs and lows of adult life. Depending on the institution, there may be more social opportunities open to you than ever before.

I have been to both college and university. I think it's fair to say both were a whole different experience to each other. At college, I studied Animal Management. The course had its ups and downs, but I learned a lot, and most of the people I met were friendly. I don't recall there being many social events going on, however. Whether that was just the style of the college, or because I wasn't on a university-equivalent course, or me being oblivious to any events that were happening, I don't know.

University was a much more socially intense environment. After a couple of years of home study and rethinking my career path, I went to university to study Creative Writing and Journalism. During my first year, I commuted from home via train. It wasn't far, and although it put a limit on how heavily involved I could get with the social scene, that didn't bother me. University came with a lot of newness, and I needed to get used to it one stage at a time. Living independently and attending regular late-evening social events could wait.

How much you participate in the social scene depends partly on what you want to get out of it and partly on how much extra stuff you can take on in one go. Joining societies or clubs – if there are any – can be a good way of meeting fellow students with similar interests to you and finding opportunities for social events. If you want to make friends or learn new skills outside of what your course has to offer, then it may be worth stepping out of your comfort zone a little to meet new people and try new things. This will probably get easier once you know a few people. What's important, though, is that you get through it at your own pace, and if you need a few weeks to get to know people or find extracurricular activities, that is absolutely fine. Here are some pointers to bear in mind, especially while you are new:

- Get an idea of **what sort of things are likely to be happening.**
- Think about **what sort of activities you might be interested in** and how much time and energy you have.

- **Learn how to say no** to things you don't want to do or can't realistically manage.
- **Learn how to make the most of opportunities you do take**, including making friends.
- **Don't feel like you have to rush into joining societies** and other social groups.
- **Be open and matter-of-fact about autism** if you feel able – remember points from Chapter 1.
- **Look for opportunities that might interest you.**
- **Don't take on more than you can manage** – be mindful of how much you can fit in alongside your study schedule without burning out.
- **Chat to people on your course** (when you and they are not trying to work, that is!). Whether you are eager to make lots of friends or not bothered, it's good to get comfortable with talking to your course mates, as you will be working together throughout the duration of your course.

Even in the second year onwards, I wasn't that sociable at university. I didn't feel like I had much in common with people, and I was going through a very socially anxious phase. Looking back, I think I kept people emotionally at arm's length without even fully realising it. I also didn't have much mental energy for heavy socialising outside study times, especially in my final year. I was constantly peopled out, yet lonely at the same time, something that Naomi also struggled with:

> *"I actually ended up dropping out in my second year because of the social scene. It wasn't for me at all, and I ended up feeling incredibly isolated and anxious. I switched to the open university so I could study without having to worry about keeping up with the social culture."*

As disheartening as that may sound, that does not mean that socialising will inevitably be a nightmare. I might not have been the life and soul of the party at university, but I talked to my course mates and got on well with them. I met up with some of them in my spare time and even shared a flat with one of them (and some students on a different course) for a year. And many people thrive socially at college or university and form solid, long-lasting friendships. Several autistic people I know enjoyed the social scene and quickly bonded with the people they were with, as described later in the chapter.

The truth is that further education, with all its pros and cons, is a real mixed bag. This may be particularly true for anyone with different support needs. No two people's experiences will be the same, and it is unlikely to be all good or all bad. Both Thomas and Will felt out of their depths at times, to begin with, but still managed to have fun and connect with other people.

> *"I met quite a few people that I didn't particularly gel with, but the excitement of the whole charade was too sweet to miss. I spent 3-4 nights at clubs and events, but once the hype died down, I was back to my regular routine. [...] I joined clubs but struggled to fit in and make proper friends. [...] On a whim, I convinced my friend to attend a local flat party, and that's where I met my now best friend. We both struggled with relationship issues and mental health, so we supported each other, and she remained as the main source of light in my life."* – Thomas.

> *"I guess I didn't get to enjoy the social side as much as I could have because I was in a long-distance relationship at the time, which got in the way. I did enjoy hanging out with like-minded individuals and getting through it together with them. It was nice to be in the presence of similar people, strong individuals, who knew what they wanted to achieve."* – Will.

If you can get to know the people who you will see on a regular basis, then you are off to a good start. Enjoy the social events you take part in, but don't let them burn you out. Just focus on getting to know people and establishing your new routine, and see how your social life can work around that.

Support

> *"Support was pretty limited, but it was there when I needed it. For exams, I had someone to write out my answers for me. What I also got from my Disabled Students Allowance was my computer and the Dragon app, a form of speech recognition software, but that didn't work out for me, so I just typed my answers in the end. One of my lecturers was also a Disabled Students Coordinator. He was a very nice man who I could always talk to if I had any concerns."* – Will.

If you have an official autism diagnosis, you may well be entitled to support in some form. Exactly what sort of support is available to you will depend on the institution. This is worth taking into account if you are looking at different colleges or universities. Most places will have individuals or services to help disabled students access support. If so, there should be information about these on the college/university website, as well as any relevant contact details. You will need to familiarise yourself with what is available to you and how best to access it. If possible, ask someone who already studies there whether the advertised support actually materialises and how effective it is.

Unfortunately, not all autistic students get the support they need. For Naomi, this made university really hard:

> *"Sadly, I was not diagnosed when I attended university. I didn't even know myself then that I was autistic, so I had no support. I fully suspect that had I had support, my experience would have been incredibly different, and I may have been able to stick it out. I actually had a good*

friend at university who was autistic and had a lot of support, and they were brilliant for her. It's definitely worth seeking out disability services and checking out universities that have a good disability support service."

Still, others, like Kathleen, choose to go without support:

"I didn't really like telling anyone I was autistic. Because of this, I probably didn't get the support I needed. I managed without it and got a good degree, but perhaps I could have done even better with more support."

For me, at college, it was fairly simple. I was entitled to 25% extra time to finish assignments, and I had a Learning Support Assistant (LSA) in both years I was there. Their job was to take notes, help me with coursework, and listen to any concerns I had. They also liaised between tutors to make sure the teaching methods were adapted suitably for me. I had one session a week with them where I could work on anything I needed. In lectures and practical lessons, they not only took notes but also helped me make sense of anything I didn't understand. College wasn't always easy, but I had a good support system.

At university, there was a bit more available to me. I was given a laptop, a Dictaphone (a sort of voice recorder), and various people taking notes in my lectures, seminars, and workshops. I only used my laptop for assignments and never got very good at using my Dictaphone. I understand, however, that being able to type notes or record lectures may be hugely beneficial to people who struggle with writing, as Will found. Notetakers were also helpful in this respect. For me, the most helpful thing about having a notetaker was having someone else to make notes and understand what was going on. If there were any important notes I missed, I could always compare what I had written to what they had. Similarly, if there was anything in the lecture I didn't understand, I could always ask them immediately afterwards.

I also had a different mentor in each year. Overall, this was probably the form of support I benefitted from the most. I have stayed in touch with my first mentor, Laurie, who has contributed many insights to this book. Laurie is also autistic, which I think helped me a lot. I met up with them several times throughout the week to go over any university related concerns or just to catch up. If I had any social or academic challenges, they were pretty good at helping me figure out how to solve them. If during our meetings, I was feeling drained or didn't have much to talk about, they understood and didn't take it personally. There is a lot to be said for having a mentor with the same neurotype as you!

If you can form a good relationship with your mentor – and they are quick to understand you – they will be a valuable source of support throughout your study experience. In my first year at university, Laurie was a shining example of this, and describes the importance of this from personal experience:

> *"I had two mentors, although not at the same time. My first mentor saw me through the first two years, and I didn't really like her. She was about 26 and a hardcore feminist, which made me really uncomfortable. [...] [My second mentor] was brilliant. He was about 30 and just did stuff, which made it much easier to relate to him. He [...] stopped me from having many a panic attack. [...] It was [he] who told me I could do group work on my own, which was a fantastic relief."*

A mentor can help you figure out how to solve your problems from an impartial perspective. They can help you organise your work so that starting it feels less daunting. If you are having ongoing struggles in lectures, seminars, or workshops, they can bridge any gaps in communication between you and your lecturers. They may even be a good source of emotional support, as Thomas found when struggling with mental illness:

> *"[My student support officer] supported me with my mental health a lot and took a lot of the stress off me when deadlines passed before my eyes.*

> *Find someone who gets you and is willing to support you through those rough times. They don't have to be an autism expert to listen to you and offer a helping hand."*

If you require more emotional support than a mentor can provide, many universities and colleges have a counselling service available. When you are having a hard time with stress, mental health, or recent difficult events, counselling can make a lot of difference. Being able to talk about your problems confidentially to someone who is not otherwise involved with your life can help your head feel clearer and help you figure out how to manage your problems. I had counselling after university for a while, so I can vouch for this. And counselling at college or university is a sensible service to have. Mental illnesses are common in young adults, especially those with autism. Studying is stressful. So is living independently for the first time. It can feel like there is a lot of pressure to do well socially as well as academically. With all that in mind, good counselling can make things just that bit easier.

Having said that, not all counselling services are perfect. When I was having a hard time during my second year at university, I decided to try my university's counselling service. Students were entitled to a certain number of counselling sessions, and there didn't seem to be any rules about who could and couldn't have them. The first two or three times went pretty well, I thought. I would think about some of the things I was struggling with that I could make a note of in advance, then talk about them in a quiet space, one to one, with an older adult.

Unfortunately, a few sessions in, things took a downturn. I was feeling particularly unhappy about my autism and my sexuality, and my social anxiety was through the roof. I had several recent struggles in mind that I wanted my counsellor to help me through. When I arrived for what ended up being my final session, however, he told me that this wasn't just a drop-in service and that I shouldn't keep coming back so often when there was nothing really wrong, and my mental health seemed fine. I felt so small and ashamed; I had a shutdown and couldn't bring myself to talk about anything, no matter how hard he tried to find something. Needless to say, it was a very uncomfortable hour, and I did not come back again.

Despite my humiliating experience, I am well aware that student counselling can be a really great thing for some people. As I said, it is in a quiet place with one older adult and no one else, where you can talk about things that you have had time to think about in advance. For me, that is the ideal situation for a conversation. I think part of the reason my counsellor was so dismissive during my last session was because I presented myself at my best during the first few sessions. If this applies to you, you can tell your counsellor this at the beginning.

If you are thinking about trying university counselling, here are some tips to bear in mind:

- **Establish what you want from it,** e.g. listening, advice, problem-solving.
- **Ask the counsellor what and who university counselling is mainly for**. That way, you can get a sense of whether or not it is for you.
- **Express any worries about potential awkwardness**. It's important to be able to be honest with a counsellor about your thoughts and feelings.
- **Ask other people about their experiences with it**, especially if they have sought counselling to deal with struggles similar to yours.

To summarise, there is no guarantee that every support service available will work for you, but they are always worth looking into.

At college, I sometimes worried that the extra support I received was cheating. I still aspired to be as neurotypical as possible and was not ready to accept how disabling it is to have different needs to most of my peers. As one of my lecturers said at the time, "You're not cheating by accepting help; you're entitled to it!" I'm still not good at accepting help to this day, but it is a principle that I will try and practise as well as preach!

Studying

> *"Exams that put a focus on facts and diagrams were where I really flourished, but in a lot of cases, I was left constantly confused about what they wanted me to say. [...] Deadlines were even worse; with multiple things to do, high anxiety, and no executive functioning skills, I had a tough time. Thankfully, I formed a great relationship with my student support officer."* – Thomas.

As Thomas' experiences show, autism can have a lot of pros and cons when it comes to studying. On the one hand, we have to make sense of a whole new routine and a lot of new information. Regular interaction with people is a big part of college and university, even without lots of social activities. On the other hand, we are often dedicated to researching subjects that are important to us and also thrive on rules and routine. Traits like this can give us a major head start in pursuing our area of interest.

There are many different aspects of studying, and the exact nature of the sort of studying you will have to do will depend on your course. There will be some hours during the day when you will be expected to attend lectures, seminars, or workshops. I think it is fair to say that nearly all university and college courses will involve these in some form. The advantage of them is that they happen according to a schedule. The tricky part is retaining all the information. If someone is talking at me at length, I find it really hard to distinguish between the relevant and irrelevant points, especially when I am struggling to filter out background chatter or other noise. I am aware that many autistic people also struggle with certain types of light and have to wear sunglasses or tinted prescription glasses in places like lecture theatres, laboratories, and computer rooms.

These days, lecturers often use slideshows or documents on a projector, which makes note-taking easier as you can see the most important points. Your lecturer will probably even make any slideshows or documents available for you online or give you a printed copy. Meanwhile, talk to them about any of the following issues you experience: difficulty with eye contact, difficulty keeping up with group discussions, sensory sensitivity, and anything they need to know about what helps and hinders your concentration. That way, they can make any adjustments they can and also understand how you learn best.

When studying on your own, you have more control over your environment. The downside is you need to take more responsibility for using your time productively. Thomas has struggled with this in the past and has come out the other side with some good advice:

> *"I wrestled a lot with how much work I should be doing. Sometimes I'd burn out, and other times I slacked off too much. [...] Talk to your lecturers, support office, or disability service team and devise a study plan together. Study with your friends or course mates. That way, you have a bit of social pressure to get you out of the house. Scan your campus for different studying spots, find your favourites and move between them throughout the day. That way, you can break up your day better and stop yourself from going insane with boredom."*

This illustrates another important point: while there will always be uncomfortable sensory stimuli to deal with, you can at least choose when, where, and with whom to work. At both college and university, I preferred to work alone in the library. Wherever you prefer to work, you can create a study space that gets you in the right mindset for working. To do this, you need to keep all the basic things you need close at hand – stationery, notes, reading material, a bottle of water, and anything to manage sensory overload, such as earphones or tinted glasses.

Getting started on the work itself can be the hardest part. Kathleen describes how it feels for her, and for many of us on the spectrum, when under pressure to conquer a challenge alone:

> *"I felt I didn't do as well as I could have done when it came to essay writing. I struggle with planning academic work. I [...] get really intimidated by the idea of beginning a task. To combat this, I often dive in immediately and feel an urge to just get it over with, which means I'm probably not as thorough as I need to be."*

Most big tasks will feel less daunting when broken down into smaller tasks (as I am discovering with writing this book!). With an essay, you can divide your main topic (let's pretend it's autism in adulthood!) into sections (e.g. explaining autism, data overload, friendships, etc.), then divide each of those into points you want to cover (e.g. what autism means, how to tell people, etc.). That way, you have essentially given your essay a skeleton, as shown in the cartoon sketch at the beginning of this chapter. With revision, divide your working day into chunks of time dedicated to a certain subject, with the subjects you find the hardest taking priority.

This brings me onto my next point: time management. Whatever kind of studying you are doing, you need to figure out what kind of schedule works for you and how you can divide your time fairly between all your assignments. If you are easily bored or distracted, lots of short study periods may be best. If, on the other hand, you are prone to hyper-focusing, be firm with yourself about working on the same thing for a set amount of time and no more so that you are able to give your time and energy to everything you are working on that day. Either way, remember to also take a short break in between each study period. Take the time to eat, drink, go to the toilet, move around, and have a change of scene. As a result, your mental energy levels will probably last longer, and you'll be fitting in basic self-care too.

And finally, exams. I cannot emphasise this enough: be clear about when and where they are happening! If the exam times are online, keep checking them, and double check with a member of staff or fellow student the day before. My only university exam got off to a terrible start when the online change in the start time passed me by, and I turned up nearly an hour late. I had it in my head that it was at ten and missed the update because I have never been good at retaining information that I am not personally alerted to and in a hectic class environment. To cut a long story short, I was allowed to re-sit at a later date, but I am aware that I got off very lightly here.

With a bit of luck, if you are registered as having extra support needs, you may take exams in a separate room from your peers, with fewer people. You may find it less overwhelming that way, but if you have any sensory sensitivities you are worried about, talk to a member of staff about it well in advance. Once you are in there, you can treat the exam paper similarly to a study schedule and try to spend roughly the same amount of time on each section. It is better to answer all or most of the questions well enough than to spend so much time trying to answer one perfectly that you don't have time to finish all of them. My stepfather John is a university academic. He says if only students knew how easy it is to get the first 30% of marks for any question just by producing the beginnings of an answer that is mostly correct and relevant to the question. The same amount of time spent trying to perfect an answer you have already spent too long on is highly unlikely to gain you more than 5%. You can always go back to earlier questions if you have time at the end.

Group projects and practical work

When I was at college, the animal management course I was doing comprised 40% practical lessons. In hindsight, I'm not sure why knowing this in advance was not enough to make me wonder whether or not this course was right for me. Sure enough, practicals were difficult. Herding sheep or pigs from one space to another meant having to move quickly and in the right direction without getting knocked over. Cleaning and tidying farm animal enclosures with brooms and shovels required a surprising amount of hand-eye coordination. All practicals involved instinctively being able to keep up with what other people were doing while still focusing on the task at hand. In other words, many practical lessons were dyspraxia hell. Although I passed the whole course with distinctions, it was my dyspraxic attempts at practical work that made me think that perhaps I was not on the right career path!

Despite the lack of physical labour, Journalism practicals in my final year at university were not much better. Our main Journalism assessments were group projects, and it's fair to say that tensions ran high the whole time. One project involved creating a business plan for a magazine. Another involved writing and designing another magazine. Both involved having to keep up with what other people were doing and expected me to do, ambiguous, changeable communication from different people, tasks and goals changing spontaneously, tension between group members, and stress that escalated as we approached deadlines. Not surprisingly, the overload of ambiguous communication, the mix of task and emotion-focused behaviour, and the copious social interaction required left me exhausted and bewildered. I would do a load of work that turned out to be a waste of time because the plans had changed without me knowing. I couldn't always identify what to do; my course mates didn't know how to communicate with me, and, as ever, I ended up on the sidelines.

Practical work in any form can easily become a nightmare for autistic students. We are often single-minded in our approach to getting a task done, we are easily overstimulated, and we are constantly fighting through a mismatch of communication between ourselves and our neurotypical colleagues. As with many autistic people, my friend Naomi took the academic side of her work very seriously and felt at odds with students who were more interested in social interaction:

> *"I struggled when it came to group work [...]. I found that people would rely on me to do the majority of the academic side and then end up taking the credit for it. I was often ahead because I was so interested in my studies and then got bored in lectures and seminars because I'd already read the stuff. [...] I found that university was way more about the socialising and was very disappointed. That is worth autistic people taking into account before going."*

The trick to getting through tasks where you are out of your depth is to identify your natural working style and figure out how to incorporate it into the task at hand. If you are most productive when given a chunk of work to do alone, make this clear to your course mates and lecturer, and offer to take on tasks that can easily be done by one person. If you thrive on repetitive work, try looking out for more mundane tasks that most people find tedious.

On top of all that, make sure the people you are working with, including your lecturer, are aware of what autism means for you when working with other people. You can tell them in writing or in person. Even if you choose the latter, you might find it helpful to write it down first so you can be clear with yourself about what you want to say. For example:

- I might ask you to explain things to me on a one-to-one basis to make sure I've understood correctly.

- I might find it hard to keep up with important points raised in a group discussion where people might be talking at the same time, wording things in a way that is confusing for me, changing or contradicting previously established points, and bringing up lots of information all at once.
- I work best when given a clear set of instructions and my own space and time to work.
- I will find it bewildering when I am corrected for something I didn't know was wrong. Please explain where I have gone wrong in a concise, logical way, without getting angry or impatient.
- If we have to assess each other's contribution, please remember that a group of people in which lots of information is thrown around is not a very autism-friendly situation. This doesn't mean that I should be given extra credit when I haven't earned it, but assessing each other's work may highlight areas I have found particularly confusing or things I was unaware of.

In short, use your autistic traits to your advantage in an otherwise challenging environment, and try to make people aware of how you function best. Group work and practical labour may not always be that simple, but you can give yourself a head start if you know what to expect.

Accommodation and house sharing

There are several different options for college or university accommodation. If you already live a short journey away from where you study, you can commute from home. Most institutions have halls of residence, which for many students is a good way of transitioning from living with their family to living completely independently. Whether things like catering and cleaning are included or not will vary among different halls, so it is important to know what you want and what the halls you are looking into provide.

I first moved out of my parents' house for my second year at university. At that point in my life, I had just had a mostly very successful first year and was feeling pretty optimistic about how the next two years would be. It did not occur to me to be worried about taking care of the privately rented flat I was moving into because I knew how to clean and cook. I had some reservations about how my then housemate and I would get along while living under the same roof, but I brushed them off.

I should have known that this was one of those times when reality would fall short of expectations when we were cleaning the flat before moving in, and I discovered a well-concealed compartment in the fridge full of putrid, rotting food. It appeared to be curry sauce, mayonnaise, garlic, and chocolate, but given that it was decomposing before my eyes, it was hard to be sure. I had no idea how many months or years it had been quietly decomposing in the fridge, but it could not stay there any longer. My housemate and I donned our rubber gloves, disposed of the food while trying not to be sick, and gave the fridge a very thorough scrubbing. I was glad that I already knew basic cleaning skills but a little disappointed by the hygiene standards in this place.

Cleanliness is a common issue in student accommodation, whether it's mess left by previous tenants or current tenants' lack of motivation or cleaning skills. You would be well advised to learn basic things such as washing dishes, polishing different surfaces, dusting, and vacuuming if you haven't already. It is also worth giving your new house or flat a thorough clean before you move in. Accommodation that is specifically for students may have someone who cleans the place before anyone moves in, but even then, you might want to have one last look at the place before you move in.

You will also need to learn other practical skills, such as food shopping and cooking (unless you are being catered for), laundry, online banking, and creating a routine for all of the above so that you stay on top of them. If you are not already used to them, the weeks and months before moving out are the best time to practise with help from your family. I say this because, for many autistic people, myself included, learning skills outside our comfort zone can be daunting. Despite being very hygiene conscious, I never got very good at cleaning a bathroom or kitchen. I know that Kathleen had similar struggles with practical skills when house sharing:

> *"I struggled with a lot of the practical aspects of living away from home. Things like cooking and understanding money etc., are things I find difficult […]. It was hard as my housemates at uni didn't understand this […]. Although we often joked about me being 'bad at life', sometimes it upset me that my friends may have thought I was incompetent, naive, or sheltered. I wanted to explain that being autistic may have played a part in this, but I […] didn't want to use it as an excuse. Looking back, I wish I stood up for myself a bit more."*

Another good way to prepare is to plan well in advance what sort of things you might need to have in your accommodation. You will need to take into account what you will be bringing from home and what you will need to buy. These will likely include furniture, décor, cooking utensils, and things that will need replacing, such as food and cleaning products. Homeware shops will often have good deals and discounts, especially in the lead up to the start of the academic year when many students will be moving out for the first time. You can also ask people you know if they have any homeware items they no longer need that still work that they would be willing to donate to you. There is no guarantee that you will get much stuff this way, but if you do, then great!

Then there is the issue of housemates. Whether you choose them or not depends on your living arrangements. If you are moving into student halls, you may be able to choose some or all of your housemates, or you may be put with anyone. With other rented accommodation, you will probably need to find people to house share with. This can be hard when you are autistic. It can be one of those situations where one minute you are unsure of what to do, and the next, everyone has gone and done it without you! If asking people face-to-face isn't an option or hasn't worked, this is where social media can come in handy. You can write a post saying you are looking for housemates who are moving to the same area, and also look for groups and pages connected with your university and ask there. It might help to include a little bit about your personality and lifestyle so that you are more likely to get responses from similar people. And if you don't get any responses, it is ok to post again after a while.

If you don't already know your housemates, it might be worth getting to know them a little bit, preferably before you move in together. It doesn't matter if you don't become best friends with them, but it may be more comfortable for everyone if you don't feel like complete strangers the whole time. Besides, you all need to know what you are getting into. Could you live with someone who is untidy or noisy? Or someone who needs a clean, quiet environment? What about someone who has very different social needs from you? Or someone who is likely to bring back lots of friends and/or a partner on a regular basis? While you are unlikely to find housemates who completely fit your ideals, you can at least learn what to expect.

This is yet another situation where it is worth explaining autism if you feel at all able. We've established how easy it is to end up on the outside in any group setting. If you experience this with a group of housemates, it may be all the more alienating when you are in such close proximity to each other. This was something that Naomi found particularly hard:

"I found house-sharing very, very difficult. I like my own space, and although I got on with everyone on the surface, I could not keep up with the amount of time they spent together, so I often felt left out. I have frankly rubbish recognition of facial expressions and social cues, so I just felt lost a lot of the time. I exhausted myself wearing my social mask and was constantly anxious."

In this case, you will need to focus on the implications of being an autistic housemate, such as:

- Any noises, smells, or foods that you cannot tolerate.
- Your strengths and weaknesses when it comes to practical and financial tasks. For example, I find working in the kitchen at the same time as someone else really stressful. I think this is because I cannot quickly read what the other person is about to do or where they are about to move, so I struggle to coordinate whatever I am doing accordingly. Trying to do so takes up concentration. I also find it hard to filter out noise and movement around me.
- Your need for routine and clear communication, if applicable.
- Your need for alone time, if applicable.
- How you might come across when stressed or overloaded.

Also, remember that no matter how well you know and like each other to begin with, living together will change the dynamics of your relationship. You won't get as much of a break from them as before, you will have to evenly share household chores, and you will end up learning a lot about each other's habits and routines. Because of this, many people advise that you do not live with your very best friend if you want to preserve that friendship just the way it is. If things go wrong between you, you don't want to be left without a close friendship to fall back on for support.

That's not to say that living with housemates is always hard. There is potential for difficulties, but also for friendship and a good understanding of each other. Will, Luna, and Kathleen enjoyed house-sharing overall and managed to find some good friends in the process:

> *"I found living with other people quite chilled and relaxed. I was comfortable with it, especially in my final year. I lived with a friend from my course and his housemates, and it was the best year of my life. They were really lovely people. I didn't have many problems with people at university. There were some who were very hot-headed, but they weren't horrible or bad people; it was just the way they were. Overall, at university, it was really nice."* – Will.

> *"[Living with other people was] good because they were friendly, like a family. They looked after me and encouraged me to cook from a recipe book."* – Luna.

> *"[…] I was really lucky, as my flatmates and I got on really well, and we all went to social events together. We became close friends quickly and decided to live with each other for the next few years. We're still friends now. […] I finally felt I could be myself and walk around without feeling self-conscious."* – Kathleen.

Even if you don't form lasting friendships, it is enough to be able to co-operate and get on with your housemates without feeling alienated. New accommodation can take weeks to get used to but having the right skills and the right people can help you to feel more settled.

Graduation

> *"I felt like a fool because some students said, 'I bet you will trip when you shake hands.' This stayed in my mind and made me self-conscious. I did trip."* – Luna

Luna's experience summarises many students' worst nightmare about their graduation day. In the lead up to my university graduation, many of my course mates were nervous about the actual ceremony, when we would be called on stage in front of hundreds of people. For me, this was the least of my worries. I would be sitting in the audience for most of it, and when I would need to go on stage, it would be for only a few minutes to go through a clear, well-rehearsed ritual.

If only the rest of the day was that straightforward.

I was surrounded by people for a whole day, constantly aware of the feel of the summer sun and my graduation gown and hat (once I was wearing them), and under a lot of pressure to be sociable and act excited. There were ambiguous expectations about when and where to go for clothes and photos. I had to be on constant high alert for social cues as I tried to figure out where to wait, when to move forward and how far, and how to interact with the staff in a neurotypical way. Even when I wasn't expected to go to a certain place at a certain time, there was so much noise and activity; it was impossible for me to focus. I had to maintain my neurotypical mask enough to mingle with my course mates and make small talk with the people accompanying them. To top it off, I also had to deal with the occasional passer-by saying to me, 'Smile, it's your graduation ceremony!' as, unbeknownst to them, I steadily descended further into shutdown mode.

Thankfully, my mum noticed I was having a shutdown and was able to ask a member of staff to find a quiet space for just the two of us. I think I had been putting so much effort into processing everything that was going on, I hadn't even realised I was having a shutdown until I started to feel more human. The ceremony came and went; we had one last round of photos, and before I knew it, the day was over. This was just as well because I had no mental energy to spare.

How much sensory overload you have to endure on your graduation day – if you have one – will depend partly on the location. A noisy, heavily built-up city may feel busier than somewhere more rural. A quieter, more spacious environment meant that Kathleen's graduation ceremony was fairly peaceful and straightforward as these things go:

> *"I enjoyed my graduation ceremony. [My university] was in a very peaceful, idyllic place, so there were not many sensory issues for me. The ceremony took place in a town hall, with a celebration outside afterwards, so it didn't feel too crowded or overwhelming."*

I think it is important for people to understand that for some students, a graduation ceremony isn't going to be all fun and games. I'm sure I'm not the only person who thinks this. There are bound to be other people with disabilities, illnesses, or other personal struggles that make such an occasion exhausting to have to deal with, especially with limited understanding from other people. With that in mind, I'll list a few pointers that I wish had occurred to me in the lead up to my graduation.

- **Ask someone in charge what to expect in advance** – a step by step explanation of what is going to happen, what you need to do, and where you need to go, complete with times.
- **Talk to a member of staff at your university** about any concerns you might have. Ideally, talk to someone you know and get on well with, such as one of your lecturers or a member of support staff. Even if they can't help directly, they may be able to recommend someone who can.
- **Find out in advance if there is anywhere quiet you can go** if it gets overwhelming.
- **Bring anything that will help you stay calm** to use in a quiet moment.

Meanwhile, Thomas has his own advice for getting through graduation:

> *"Don't feel any expectation to do anything social. Everybody is distracted and placing a super high priority on getting the best pictures. Thank the staff who helped you on your journey, get a few pictures with your mates, then go and chill. The actual ceremony is [...] incredibly long and tedious. If you don't feel comfortable sitting amongst the crowd of graduates, ask an authority figure if you can sit somewhere else. [...] Bring some noise-cancelling headphones for good measure, as there can be a lot of people and loud noises."*

The thing to remember is that a graduation ceremony is supposed to be a special day. Whilst a bit of sensory or social discomfort may be hard to avoid, you have a right to do whatever you need to do to make it manageable – and even enjoyable!

CHAPTER 6

The Working Environment

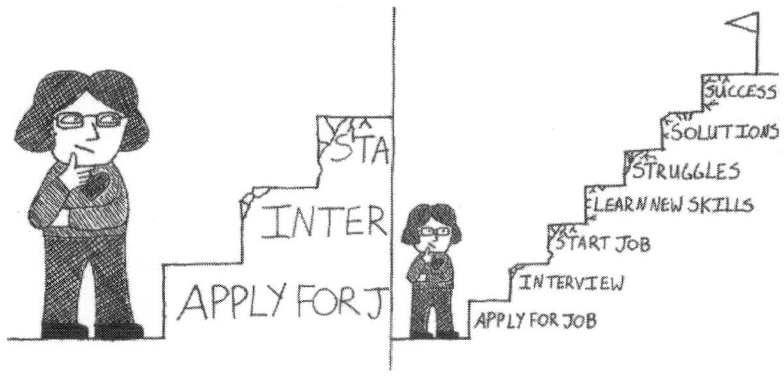

According to *Autism Equality in the Workplace* by Janine Booth (page 16),[4] only 15% of autistic adults are in full-time employment. In addition, 43% of autistic adults have had to leave a job because of autism-related struggles, and 37% have never had a paid job. That's a pretty grim set of statistics to start the chapter with.

Why do autistic people often have such a hard time finding and keeping a job? The short answer is systemic bias. In other words, most working environments will have been created by and for neurotypical people, no matter how seriously they take disability rights. People are expected to communicate in a neurotypical way. Those who do will have an easier time learning the job and are also more likely to be understood and taken seriously. The physical environment is often built for neurotypical people's sensory comfort (though I realise there are some jobs that aren't comfortable for anyone). Autistic people, meanwhile, are vulnerable to implicit and explicit discrimination and even bullying, as Laurie and Luna have both found:

> *"I've faced so much prejudice and discrimination, mainly from people who should have known better. I've faced some utterly dehumanising situations and dreadful treatment that, at times, has been seen as a reasonable adjustment yet showed total lack of understanding of autism."* – Laurie.

> *"One place I worked in was an afterschool club. The leader said I seemed different. She used to shout at me for not remembering instructions. This caused other children to do the same. The eldest child, aged about nine, said, 'Shall we form a hate Luna group?'"* – Luna.

I'll be honest, I haven't had as much work as a lot of people my age, and what I have had has had some pretty drastic ups and downs. I have struggled to work quickly or retain new information. I have forgotten or misinterpreted rules. I have had to ask people to explain things to me more clearly. I have reached milestones that I had to push myself for, only to be laid off anyway. I have burned myself out from trying to find ways to overcome things I found difficult.

On a more positive note, I have also passed a job probation through finding my own ways of learning when it seemed inevitable that I would fail. I have stayed in the same job long enough to become one of the most senior members on the team. I have trained new people. I have been trusted with major solo projects that have benefitted my colleagues. I have had much appreciation from customers after being able to help them. As much as I might be bragging here, this isn't the intention. What I'm trying to say is that despite the setbacks that many autistic people face at work, it won't always be hard.

Job hunting

Finding a job is the first step! It is one of those tasks that may sound so simple and yet is full of ambiguity. How do you 'find' or 'get' a job? Where do you look? What do you actually have to do?

While employment itself is hard to come by at the time of writing, job vacancies may be easier to find than ever before, thanks to modern technology. If you type what sort of job you are looking for and the desired location (e.g. shop jobs in York) into Google, any vacancies that fit those criteria will come up. There are also many job vacancy websites out there that you can browse and even subscribe to by email. A few UK examples are CV Library, Jobrapido, Indeed, Glassdoor, and Google for Jobs. The application process will vary slightly with different job vacancies and job websites, but you will generally be required to submit your name, address, contact details, details of your education and any previous work experience, and your CV.

You may find you are eligible for disability employment services. These will vary but can include career options counselling, guidance with CV writing, job hunting, and interviews. They are also there to offer support when it comes to disability accommodation and discrimination.[5] The advantage of job hunting this way is that these programs are specifically designed for people with different needs and can support you through disability-specific issues at work in a way that many companies won't.

Getting an interview

Whichever way you go about job hunting, you can bet it is going to be a slow process, and you may have to apply for jobs every day for weeks or even months before you are invited to an interview. If and when you are, congratulations! You have reached the next step. When you get invited to a job interview, the expectations for the interview process will usually be made clear to you in advance. The person inviting you will probably advise you on when to arrive and what time the interview is due to start. If there is anything you are unsure about, you should be able to email your interviewer(s) in advance.

There are several things that you need to do or think about beforehand; however, that will not be made clear to you. For such a short task, job interviews require a surprising amount of effort in how you present yourself. In order to make an impression on your interviewers, you need to not just answer their questions but show that you understand the job you are being interviewed for. To manage this, you will need to research the job and the company (i.e. what they do, what their goal is, and how they operate). For example, if you are applying for any kind of retail job, you will need to have at least a basic knowledge of the company's products and products like them in general.

Once you have a basic understanding of the job and the company, you will need to think of one or two questions to ask at the end of the interview based on what you have read that you think they could tell you more about. You could ask about how they do a certain task or how they have achieved a recent accomplishment. Or how they keep up with what customers/clients want from them. Or how current or recent national/international events are impacting their work. Brexit, perhaps? Or the COVID-19 pandemic? It's hard to offer any specific examples here because this depends so much on the exact job, but I hope this gives a rough idea of how to prepare.

You will also need to be able to tell your interviewers why you think you would be good for the job. This is what employers want to know when they ask you what you think you could bring to this job. They don't mean your backpack, lunch, and water bottle! Make a note beforehand of your positive personality traits, paying particular attention to the ones that would be good for this job and the reasons why. While lying isn't a good idea, you may have to exaggerate a little. This isn't the time to be modest; you need to tell them what makes you stand out as a potential employee. Think about your accomplishments in the academic and working environment that are relevant to this particular job. Be prepared to talk about why your experiences with them would make you a good candidate for the job. For example, if you are applying for a job in a shop, it will be worth mentioning any experiences where you have provided good customer service and how you did it. If you are applying for an editing or copywriting job (as I have done), you will probably be expected to talk about a situation where you have used your editing skills.

Explaining autism at work

As with telling anyone about autism, there are many possible advantages to telling your employers and colleagues; and a few risks. The stakes may feel higher than disclosing it in a more day to day situation; telling could lead to people trying to support you and create a safe, positive working environment, or it could lead to people assuming you are not capable, and unfortunately, there is only so much you can do to explain to them in a positive yet realistic way. I realise that this will vary depending on your strengths and the nature of the job, but it is an important thing to consider. In the UK, you are not legally obliged to disclose your autism. If you do, however, there will be certain legal rights accessible to you. It will be easier for you to prove any discrimination or harassment you experience. Your employers will have a legal obligation to make any reasonable adjustments for you – that is, make modifications to your working environment to the extent that they can reasonably be expected to ensure that your needs are met and that you will be treated fairly.[6]

Also, there may well be people who are prepared to listen and learn from you and support you in whatever way you need. Thomas and Naomi have faced mistreatment from others but have also managed to connect with people who have been kind and helpful:

> *"Some colleagues can be amazing, shining examples of kindness and understanding. You have to get to grips with the fact that most people don't understand you. Instead of brooding over that fact, be confident about being autistic and seek to educate others if they ask about it. [...] Cherish those who want to understand you."* – Thomas.

> *"I find it helpful when somebody asks me how [autism] affects me or even just lets me know that it's ok to tell them when I find something difficult. The best thing is the few precious people who basically treat me the same and value me the same when they know. These are the people I can tell if I'm struggling, and they don't look down on me but try and support me. I can probably count these people on one hand, and I treasure them greatly!"* – Naomi.

It is important to give anyone interviewing or employing you a brief outline of things you want them to be aware of on your CV, during job interviews, and when you start a new job. Explaining on a CV and during an interview doesn't need to be complicated – it just needs to include things that you need them to understand right from the start. Employers and potential employers need to understand why you might come across differently and how they can best communicate with you. I have listed examples of autistic traits that I think they need to be aware of when it comes to first impressions:

- I may be uncomfortable with eye contact or not know when and how to use it. A lack of eye contact does not mean I am not listening – I may actually find it easier to listen when I am not making eye contact.

- I may not be naturally expressive in body language, face, or voice – this does not mean a lack of interest.
- I may ask for some questions or statements to be clarified or rephrased.
- I may need clear, literal communication, with any extra details given after the main question or statement, instead of being mixed up with it.
- I may sometimes interpret questions or statements literally. If you ask me a question that could be interpreted in more than one way, please specify what sort of answer you are looking for.

You will also need to emphasise your autistic traits that will potentially give you an advantage with your work. If you have extensive knowledge of the sort of work you are doing, or any subject relevant to it, then that is definitely worth mentioning. Being detail-oriented may serve you well in a number of different jobs. Being structured and methodical may be an advantage when doing repetitive tasks that some people might find boring. Being a very visual thinker will give you a head start in design or photography. Having a good vocabulary and use of grammar will be a strength when it comes to written work.

When you start a job, as well as re-emphasising your strengths, you will need to explain in more detail some of the things you struggle with that your boss and colleagues need to be aware of. For example:

> *"I find having someone sitting down and giving me a long in-person explanation of how something works very difficult, although I realise sometimes this is unavoidable. I personally prefer being given tasks over email, so I don't feel pressure to nod along, look interested, and make the right noises ('yes,' 'mm hmm', 'great', etc.)."* – Kathleen.

> *"There's something in the unspoken or the nuance that I totally miss. I've found it helpful to be able to shadow a colleague closely and, perhaps, for longer than others. It's hard to ask for that, and somehow, we need to get across to employers and colleagues that if we can do that, our competence will excel. It's not slowness and stupidity; it's a dedication to accuracy and detail. It's like we are not equipped to 'muddle through' like I think so many neurotypical brains do!"* – Abby.

> *"[I struggle with] people talking too fast and not explaining instructions clearly, and with feeling stupid for not understanding."* – Luna.

I have found in the past that I am more aware of what my struggles are when I have them! In other words, once I have started the job and am learning more about it. I understand this must be frustrating for employers who need to know what to expect before I start. Generally, it should be fine to explain any concerns you have once you have had a bit of time to get used to your role. You will have a better understanding of the nature of the work, and it is important to voice any concerns you have while you are still being trained. Unfortunately, you cannot control how well people understand, but making them aware will give you the best possible chance for making positive changes to your experience in the workplace.

And chances are, with enough understanding from your boss and colleagues, there will be certain areas of work where you thrive. Laurie has faced many challenges at work yet has many skills that have served them well at work.

> *"[…] In the job I was doing before going to uni, I was moved around teams a few times, which didn't always sit well with me, but I did a great job when it came to investigating the root causes of appointment failures because my autistic problem-solving ability would look below the surface and allow me to succeed where others failed."*

Similarly, my bookshop internship was good for me in many ways. Most of the tasks I was given were repetitive and methodical, and it was easy to have someone talk me through them while I was still learning. We were all encouraged to read the books when we didn't have anything else to do, in order to develop an understanding of what we were selling, which suited me just fine as a keen reader! As a result, I was often able to think of books to recommend to customers, which would leave them with a good impression of the shop as a whole.

Overcoming struggles

The working environment can be a challenging place for anyone. It can be especially difficult when you learn and communicate on a different wavelength from your colleagues. The trick is to bear in mind the nature of how you learn, what you struggle with, and the work itself, and think about how you could take a different approach to learning and getting things done. When I first got a job as a copywriter at an online retailer, I barely got through my probation. I couldn't always remember lots of different rules and instructions at once; I often didn't pick up on bits of information that were communicated alongside lots of other stuff or with a lot going on and struggled to work both quickly and accurately. My anxiety skyrocketed, and I became increasingly despondent.

I knew that if I wanted to turn things around, I was going to have to take a different approach. I took to writing down any misunderstandings between me and my colleagues, so I could pinpoint what went wrong on both sides and how to avoid problems in future. I made a list of things I still didn't know so I could ask other people about them. I made notes of things I learned so that I could refer to them at any time. I revised processes I still didn't fully understand or remember until I knew them by heart. When I had trouble learning how to do Excel formulas, I made notes from video tutorials and practised doing them outside of working hours.

Meanwhile, to decide whether or not it was worth extending my probation, my boss set me a task that involved adding images, plus additional data not included in the uploading stage, for at least 100 already uploaded products in 4 hours. I had done this many times before and still hadn't mastered speed and accuracy at the same time. I had an idea and only one chance to try it. I would aim to do 12-13 products by 30 minutes, 25 by an hour, 50 by 2 hours, and 100 by 4 hours. In other words, aim for a series of small targets rather than one big target, thus ensuring that I was working at a consistent speed. My brain was exhausted by the end, but I managed just over 100, and my accuracy was better than it had ever been before.

It's hard for me to advise in any more detail than that because everyone's learning style is different. So is every kind of work, and I realise that what helped me may not help everyone. This is just one example of how it's always worth trying to find ways of managing these things.

A common problem autistic adults face at work is differences in communication styles. This can include struggling to keep up in a group discussion, picking up on implications, and knowing when and how to speak. In a big team, when I am trying to focus on getting my job done, I do not always have the mental energy for these things. Naomi has also found this tough:

> *"I generally have always managed work tasks, but the social politics of work, the gossiping and the small talk have always been exhausting for me. I think because I don't understand a lot of it, but I try very hard to fit in. I have always struggled to let colleagues know I am autistic. I have burnt myself out many times due to trying to appear socially adept when really, I'm utterly lost."*

Communication can also be an issue when being trained in new skills. When I later took on a Customer Service role in the same company, trying to understand and be understood by my colleagues was not easy. My new boss told me that there was no right or wrong answer when trying to figure out how best to solve a problem for a customer. Taking this to mean it didn't matter how I solved a problem; I later grew increasingly frustrated when I kept accidentally breaking rules that I wasn't aware of. It seemed that what it actually meant was 'there are several ok ways of doing it and some less-ok ways, and you need to instinctively know which are which'.

Then there was the issue of me asking short questions and getting long and confusing answers. Often when I asked what I needed to do next, someone would give me a big long explanation of what we were doing or why. It wasn't that I thought these details were unimportant. It's just that I was not asking what the task was or why we were doing it. I needed to understand first and foremost what I needed to do and how to do it.

To combat this issue, I wrote an explanation of the communication struggles I was having for my boss and the person training me:

> *Hello,*
>
> *As you probably know, I am autistic, which means that I sometimes learn and communicate a bit differently. Trying to learn new skills in a neurotypical dominant environment can be really frustrating and isolating, and I appreciate it when people take the time to learn how to explain things in an autism-friendly way. So I recently came up with the following analogy:*
>
> *If I ask someone, 'should I do x or y?' and they answer, 'x', that is like me asking, 'would you like tea or coffee?' and them answering, 'tea, please'.*

If I ask, 'do I need to do x?' and they answer, 'yes' or 'no, you need to do y' that is like me asking, 'is it tea you want?' and them answering, 'yes please' or 'no, coffee please'.

Sometimes I'll ask, 'should I do x or y?' and they'll ask me to do something else. That is like me asking, 'would you like tea or coffee?' and them answering, 'just water, please'. Ok, it wasn't one of the answers I was offering, but it's something I understand and can do.

Other times I'll ask, 'should I do x or y?' or 'do I need to do x?' and they'll give a lengthy explanation. That is like me asking, 'would you like tea or coffee?' or 'is it tea you want?' and them saying, 'You need to brew it so that it's not too strong, leave it for exactly three minutes, add two sugars, and some milk, as I don't like it too dark. This is my favourite drink because it's what my family always make.'

This is too confusing. When they say, 'you need to…' are they confirming that I have the right idea or correcting me? 'Brew' makes it sound like they are talking about tea, but 'dark' makes it sound more like coffee. Yes, I can count how many minutes to leave it for and how many sugars to add, but these don't tell me which drink the person wants. How much is 'some' milk? My idea of 'some' might be too much or not enough. As for this being their favourite drink, that tells me why it's important that I get this right, but it still doesn't answer my question!

If the other person answers my question directly, with no information that is not immediately required, this is easier for me to understand. They might say, 'Tea, please (or 'yes that's correct') two sugars and a splash of milk. Leave it for three minutes.' Other details may be important and/or easy to understand on their own, but these need to wait rather than be jumbled up with the information I'm asking for. Otherwise, I will struggle to discern the most important points and not retain anything. It's not that I don't want to know other details, or that I am incapable of understanding them, or that I don't think they're important. I just need them to wait until I am clear on what I need to do and how to do it.

If I ask, 'should I do x or y?' and they ask me to use my own judgement but then don't like what I have done and think I should have anticipated that, that is like me asking, 'would you like tea or coffee?' and them asking me to choose. Then when I make tea, they say, 'I prefer coffee. You should know that by now.'

Similarly, if I ask, 'should I do x?' and they say no but later get annoyed because they were expecting me to do a similar thing instead, that is like me asking, 'would you like tea?' and them saying, 'no thanks', but later getting annoyed because they were hoping I would make coffee.

If I ask, 'how should I do x?' and they say there is no right or wrong answer, but then I make a mistake because I wasn't aware of a certain rule, that is like me asking, 'how do you like your tea?' and the other person saying, 'I'm not fussy' only for me to make the tea and them to say, 'It's too weak, and you put in too much sugar.'

If it really doesn't matter how I do something, then great, but I need the other person to explicitly differentiate between that, and when there are several ok ways of doing it and some not-ok ways.

In short:

- *Say exactly what you mean.*
- *Be concise and literal.*
- *Prioritise giving the information that was asked for – try and leave other stuff until afterwards.*
- *Be aware of how frustrating, draining, and isolating struggling to communicate with neurotypicals can be, especially when I can sense people are judging me or getting impatient.*

I hope that helps and thank you for reading!

Grace

(Disclaimer: I don't like tea or coffee and therefore know sod all about how to make them!)

Sadly, this particular job did not last, in spite of my best efforts. The people who read the above letter seemed to respond well to it. I was told I would pass my probation if I met all the targets given to me. I did meet them, and when I did, at least one person told me as much. When it came to my final meeting, however, I was told I had not met all my targets and that I would not be keeping the job. And so it was that the past three months of communication struggles and pushing myself to my limits ended in tears (mine) and a prolonged burnout.

I realise this is quite a negative note to end this chapter on. Unfortunately, you have no say in the decisions your employers make. You can only try your hardest to make things work.

To summarise, here are a few pointers that I have found helpful for navigating struggles at work:

- **Make a note of things you have previously found hard** in a working environment, so you know what to look out for this time.
- **Make a list of all the areas you are struggling with** and take time to learn them.
- **Take note of communication issues you have** – both specific incidents and ongoing issues – and think about how you can avoid them AND how to explain to the other person how you need them to communicate with you.
- **Think about how you will manage a meltdown, shutdown, or anxiety attack** at work. At which point will you have to stop what you are doing? Will you be allowed to go outside or into another room for a few minutes? Will your boss be understanding if you explain to them in advance

what you need to do during a meltdown/shutdown/anxiety attack?

- **Inform your boss of any discrimination or harassment** from your colleagues. If your boss is part of the problem, you should be able to file a complaint.
- **If possible, bring along any items that will help reduce anxiety or sensory overload,** as long as they don't take up too much space or create a disruption to your work or other people's. Depending on what sort of job you have, you may be able to wear earplugs or headphones to reduce noise, dark glasses to reduce light, or have a stress ball or other fidget toy.

And this one from Thomas:

> *"Maintain a focus on talking to your boss about things, and if it all becomes too much, PLEASE reach out to autism organisations in your area. Companies and organisations don't like bad press, so they will likely enforce some action to keep you safe and happy."*

At the end of the day, you have no direct control over your work setting or the people in it. All you can do is try to make yourself heard and find your own way of learning the job.

CHAPTER 7

Being Out and About

Sensory overload

When applying on my behalf for Disability Living Allowance in 2005, my mum gave the following analogy to explain how sensory overload affects me when out and about:

> *"A neurotypical [...] brain is like a sound system with all the dials at zero. An autistic brain's 'dials' are all over the place between -10 and +10, so they are desperately unresponsive in some areas but very over sensitive in others. That means that Grace is being bombarded with what seem to her to be painfully intense experiences, but at the same time, she is missing things that she shouldn't..."*

A few years ago, I came up with my own analogy. Have you ever watched a film – or children's TV show – told from the perspective of a small animal in a world full of humans? Put them in a scenario where they are trying to navigate a busy place packed with people. They cannot focus on their destination when there are so many legs to dodge. They have to make split-second judgments about where to move when, they feel like they could get squashed at any moment, and you can bet there are beeping cars, barking dogs, lots of shouting, and any number of obstacles.

This is how I feel walking through a crowded social gathering, airport, big train station, shopping centre, shop (especially a big one, like a supermarket), or even a busy town or city. Although I don't literally see my surroundings as being bigger than me, as shown in the picture at the start of this chapter, I experience them as if they are 100 times noisier and more chaotic for me than they are for other people. I can't mentally filter everything I can hear and see. I am very easily startled by sudden touch, sound, or movement and often cannot help reacting in what many people would think is an overdramatic way. I find it hard to read people and make judgments about how and when to move, so I have to really concentrate when moving through a crowd. Crossing roads without traffic lights is even harder, and don't get me started on avoiding cyclists. Also, if someone is talking to me, I can often hear them well enough, but I'm not in the best place to give an intelligent reply because I can't filter out what I need to. On top of all that, chances are I have things I need to remember to do and/or places I am trying to get to.

Luna is also very sensitive to certain stimuli when out and about. This is how she describes it:

> *"I struggle with bad smells such as cigarette smells. I hate repetitive sounds such as stiletto high heels clip-clopping behind me. I hate people*

walking behind me as I feel they are walking in my personal space. I am clumsy and trip over lumps in the road and bump into things."

People on the spectrum are known for reacting to stimuli either more or less intensely than neurotypicals. This is a common reason for us to show attention deficit tendencies. On top of so many social rules to remember and social cues to look out for, we may also be acutely aware of everything about our environment to the point where it gets uncomfortable.

Shopping

Going shopping is one of those activities that I manage well enough while it lasts but find mentally exhausting. For a start, it will most likely come with a lot of background noise. Lots of talking and shouting. Probably some music. Maybe some traffic noises. Shopping may be a necessity, but it comes with a whole lot of sensory overload.

This can be especially hard if you experience spatial or visual sensitivity, as well as noise sensitivity. Laurie clearly describes what this feels like. While I don't often have to fight the urge to roll around on the floor, I share their envy of children who are not yet old enough to care about what people think of them!

"Because I have difficulty walking in wide, open places like shopping centres [...], having something to hold helps. [...] Ikea is a nightmare, as is anywhere where the colour or texture of the flooring changes and I literally have to feel the change in colour/texture with my foot to check it isn't a step. It's very unnerving, and I have to fight the urge to crawl along the floor. [..] I really admire autistic children who have no sense of societal expectations and can just be honest. If they're not happy, they roll around on the floor, and I'm so very envious."

For me, shopping is an example of a scenario where I get by on 'power saving mode'. It sounds simple enough in theory, but it involves trying to mentally juggle what I need to buy, which shops I need to go to and in which order, trying to find the things I need to buy, and reading other people quickly enough to avoid getting in their way, particularly when turning a corner with a shopping trolley. Then, of course, I have to pay, which in itself requires coordination and social skills: remembering what to say and quickly getting out my purse and cash or debit card while putting my shopping away.

You would think self-checkout machines would be easier because they don't require you to talk to people. If you are thinking this, let the following internal monologue demonstrate that for me, this is not the case:

> *Right, let's try the self-checkout… where does the queue start? When do I move forward? Are we supposed to move in any particular direction?... Ok, here's a machine, it says to put any bag I've brought in the bagging area… what do you mean, 'unexpected item in the bagging area'? It literally said I need to put my bag there... anyway, better start scanning… wait, why is the machine calling customer service for me? I didn't ask it to do that… finally, items all scanned… let's put the heavier things in the bottom of the bag… there are people waiting behind me, gotta hurry… I wish I could do this faster, but I only have one pair of hands… phew, all done, time to go… wait, am I not supposed to go out that way? How was I to know that?... Never mind, I'm out, time to go home…*

Self-checkout machines require you to instinctively read social cues. They say things they don't literally mean. They make a fuss the moment you break one of their ambiguous rules. They incorrectly assume you want something when you didn't explicitly ask for it and you are then wondering how the hell they reached that conclusion. In short, they are the most neurotypical devices ever invented.

When living independently, I have experimented with various tips for making shopping feel less chaotic. I can't control background noise or crowded places, but I have found ways to navigate them.

For example, when food shopping, I try to get items that come from the same aisle together to reduce how often I have to go back and forth. This gets easier once I have a rough idea of the supermarket's layout. I number the items on my list so that items in the same location have the same number. I put things on my list when I think of them, and then before I go shopping, I give the same number to all the items that are found in the same section of the supermarket. Fruits and vegetables tend to be kept together, so I would give them both the same number. Same with milk and butter. If I were well familiar with the layout of the supermarket, I would put a number 1 next to the items on my list that were closest to the entrance, number 2 next to the items that were second closest and so forth. Even if you don't go to the different sections in the order of their layout, however, you still save time if you don't have to go to each one more than once.

Example list:

- Vegetables – 1
- Lentils – 2
- Painkillers – 3
- Curry powder – 2
- Fruit – 1
- Cereal bars – 4
- Crisps – 4

- Milk – 5
- Tinned tomatoes – 6
- Tomato puree – 6
- Pasta – 7
- Hair conditioner – 3
- Noodles – 7
- Plasters – 3
- Oats – 5
- Butter – 5

With a list like this, I would get fruit and vegetables together, as they are kept in the same place in most supermarkets. I would then get lentils and curry powder. And so on.

Also, when putting items on the conveyor belt or the self-checkout bagging area, I put fruit and vegetables together along with products that are unlikely to bruise them (such as things in packets or small, light boxes), and put all those things in one bag (if I have enough shopping for more than one bag). If I have a big packet of something soft, e.g. a bag of oats, I put that at the bottom of the bag under the fruit and veg as added protection. Then I put harder things, i.e. things in cans, bottles, or heavy boxes in a separate bag. Being methodical and having a system in place makes it easier for me to focus and get the job done more quickly.

Christmas shopping is particularly draining. It's busier, the weather's likely to be unpleasant, and on top of the usual shopping struggles, I don't always know exactly what I'm getting because I have to choose presents for people based on what they like, what I can easily afford, and what's available. As a result, I find myself torn between wanting to get it over and done quickly but not wanting to leave until I find the perfect present.

It is also harder to plan for than regular grocery shopping. This is true of present shopping for any occasion, but especially so right before Christmas. You have more than one present you need to buy and there are lots of other people also out buying presents. These days, there is always the option of shopping online, but if you choose not to or are unable to, there are ways to make shopping in town less stressful. These include:

- **Asking the person/people you are buying for what sort of things they would like**, so that you have an idea of what to get before you go out. You may find this easier if you decide in advance which of those things you are going to get, possibly with a backup choice in case you are unable to buy your first choice. There is no guarantee you will find any specific thing, but you will save time if you have a plan in mind.
- **Making a note of which shops are most likely to have the item(s)** you are hoping to buy.
- **Making a list of the things you are hoping to buy and writing down which shop you are hoping to find each item in.** That way, you can decide in advance which shops you will be going to and when.
- Before you go shopping, **plan whose presents you are going to aim to buy.** Try not to leave present shopping until right before the day you give the presents so that if you are unable to buy as many presents as planned on one trip, you still have time another day.

Social gatherings

I have a love-hate relationship with social gatherings. I have attended various ones in my life, and how much I enjoy them depends on a few things. Firstly, is there anyone going who I know well? As I mentioned in Chapter 2, I'm more likely to feel comfortable socialising if I'm with a friend. Not someone I've been in the same room as before. Nor someone who recognises me who I don't recognise back. Someone I actually feel comfortable socialising with. Secondly, do I have the mental capacity for being surrounded by people right now?

As with shopping, a common struggle here is sensory overload. How can anyone focus with so much background noise? My friend Kathleen gives a good explanation of how hard this can be:

> *"I love being around my friends, but sometimes socialising is so overwhelming, and I can only deal with so much. In crowded places (bars, pubs, clubs, big family events etc.), there is so much noise it feels as though I am being stabbed in the ear over and over by voices. I like going out from time to time but often feel I need a drink or two to numb my senses slightly in order to enjoy myself. I find having music in the background can help, as it softens the chatter."*

There is also the issue of reading other people. At gatherings, people stand around in groups, then shift from one to another while I'm lingering in the background with no idea what to do. Should I go and talk to that person? How do I join in the conversation? What do I say? Then, for good measure, I might casually wander over to a group of people, wait for a pause in their conversation, only to awkwardly fade into the background again when it never comes.

I'm not much better when people come and talk to me, either. I know how to make small talk, but when I'm tired, stressed, or distracted by my surroundings, I can barely muster it up. Even when people I know talk to me, I sometimes struggle to filter out everything else I can see and hear. It's not that I'm not listening – I may well be hearing them loud and clear. It's just that I can hear too many other things loud and clear as well.

If I had an internal monologue in situations like that, it would go something like this (complete with fictional names):

> *And it's time to mingle again… should I talk to someone?… I can hear Emma and Jack talking behind me about work… I'd forgotten about her new job… wait, is that cake over there?… oh, I recognise that music!… why do children have to scream so much?… definitely cake, yay!… OH MY GOSH, someone just tapped me on the shoulder… she's trying to talk to me… no, no, it's ok, I'm fine thanks… that was so awkward, why do neurotypicals always have to touch me… kids, please shut up for a moment… was I weird? annoying? unfriendly?… should I try and catch Jane before she leaves?… oh wait, Sam is coming to chat to me… must make eye contact, but not too much… hmm, it sounds like he's had a tough week… again with the yelling, children?… now people behind me are having a loud conversation, I can't focus… what are they laughing at?… and I've lost my train of thought again…*

When you look at it like that, it's no surprise that social gatherings can get a bit much. I'm autistic and an introvert and need my space. And yet, I like to be included and to have friends. So how do I compromise? We all have our strategies, but for me, these points are key:

- **Gather the facts** about any social gathering you might be attending so you know what to expect. How long will it go on for? Who's likely to be there? What's going to happen? As obsessive as this might sound, it really helps me to form a mental picture in my head of what to expect.
- **Don't be ashamed of being socially awkward.** If I have friends or family with me, they're not going to care. Even if I don't have friends or family with me, these things are draining enough without me beating myself up internally the whole time.

- **Make it clear to people that you appreciate being included** and that having to say no sometimes to social events does not change this.
- **Take some time alone afterwards.** When you're autistic or very introverted, the only way you can present at your best in these situations is by recharging your brain afterwards.

That last point is one that I think is important for neurotypicals to understand. It's easy for people to dismiss us as antisocial or unfriendly when we need time to ourselves. The reality is that we often put so much effort and energy into our interactions with other people that we cannot keep it up without regular breaks. Below, Kathleen describes the frustration of this particular struggle:

> *"I [...] think it would just be helpful if non-autistic people could accept that some people have sensory issues and need time on their own to recover. I've experienced times when I've left a social event after one or two hours, and people are like, 'You're leaving already? Don't go!' This makes me anxious, and I worry that I've offended them by leaving early, even though I know they're trying to be nice and want to spend more time with me. [...] Sometimes even showing up takes courage/effort in itself for people who struggle with socialising."*

Travel

Travel has been a part of my life ever since I was a few months old. My mum and I would often take the plane from Taiwan to the UK to visit my grandparents before leaving Taiwan for good when I was four. With that in mind, you could say that without travel, I wouldn't be where I am today. Literally! I have been to 15 different countries by land, sea, and air throughout my life and have commuted to college, university, work experience, and work.

That is not to say that it has always been plain sailing for me, however. Quite the opposite! Adult life requires pretty much everyone to travel in some form or other. And if like me, you are an autistic, dyspraxic person, you will often find yourself at a particular disadvantage.

Driving

Driving is an important part of life for many adults. It is often seen as a coming-of-age milestone and enables people to travel distances without all the hassle of public transport. It is also a test of various physical and mental skills. There are a lot of rules to remember. You have to be able to make quick judgments about when to move. You have to be able to avoid obstacles. You have to be aware of other drivers. On top of all that, you have a steering wheel and a set of levers and pedals that you have to be able to use at exactly the right time.

Attention to detail and strict observance of rules are common autism traits that can be a real asset when driving. Abby describes her experience of this and how it may differ from a neurotypical driver's experience:

> *"I think I have a kind of hyper-vigilance when I'm driving, which is good because I observe what's going on and anticipate for quick action. I'm also a stickler for rules which is frustrating when others aren't. On the flip side, this hyper-vigilance makes me tire quite easily, and I am probably more exhausted after a drive than most."*

When I took driving lessons in my late teens, getting to grips with the car itself wasn't too hard. I drove an automatic car, which reduced the amount of multitasking I would have to do with my hands and feet, and I quickly got used to driving. What I found harder was judging what other road users were about to do. I couldn't tell when and where another driver was about to move. I couldn't read when people were about to cross the road. As a result, I was too hesitant to move when there were a lot of other road users present because I was terrified of hurting someone. My driving lessons went well enough to start with, but I never improved enough to take my driving test.

If you are considering learning how to drive, you may be able to find a driving instructor who specialises in teaching autistic people or people with disabilities in general. If you opt for a more mainstream instructor, you will need to make sure they are aware of what autism means for you when it comes to skills such as predicting other people's intentions, gross motor coordination, etc. Your instructor needs to understand how you learn and communicate and what you might struggle with, so they know how best to guide you. If you yourself are aware of any potential causes for concern, you have a good chance of overcoming your weaknesses early on.

Buses

If you do not drive, you may end up becoming a regular user of public transport. Buses are one of the most common forms of public transport, as they can travel locally, as well as over longer distances. When I got my copywriting job, it turned out to be in a location that was only accessible by bus (to a non-driver, like me). Two buses, to be precise, with the first one leaving at 7:30 am. I had almost no experience with buses back then, and there were so many things about them that I either didn't understand or learned the hard way. I didn't realise I had to wave at the driver so I could get on. Or that I had to press a button to ask the driver to stop so I could get off. I misinterpreted the ever-changing arrival time updates on the signs and gave up on many an incoming bus just because its arrival time temporarily disappeared from the electronic sign. How was I to know that the time on the sign wasn't always in sync with when the bus actually turned up?

Then, just when I thought I was beginning to get the hang of it all, the rules about printing tickets seemed to change. My monthly bus pass expired, not for the first time, and I didn't have enough cash to renew it. When I bought a regular return ticket, the driver was unable to print it and said if I explained this to the driver on the way back, they'd understand. Come home time, the bus driver I saw refused to let me on without printed evidence. The irony was this driver seemed unable to print tickets too. I had hoped that I would one day find buses as straightforward as trains. I think what actually happened was I learned to put up with their unpredictability.

For all their shortcomings, however, I can enjoy a bus ride when I know where I'm going. When I was commuting to and from work, the bus journey back was part of my unwinding time. I'd listen to my music, stare out of the window, and let my brain take a break from all the pressures of work. If my usual bus was running late, my backup bus was much slower, but it was a double-decker, which meant it was less likely to be crowded. Plus, I could listen to my music and recharge my brain on the top deck. The fact that the journey was longer meant I had more time to relax (although relaxing wasn't so easy if I needed to be home by a certain time and was unable to get the faster bus!).

Trains

I have often found trains from small train stations easier to get the hang of than buses. The platforms tend to be in a logical order, and the entrance and exit are usually easy to find. There aren't too many different trains from which to pick out the right one and the times will be clearly advertised and updated. When I commuted to my local city during my first year at university and later, my internship, the fact that the departure and arrival stations were relatively straightforward made it easier for me to learn the different stages. Buy train ticket (or scan season ticket). Go to platform 2 and wait for the fast train that stops at my destination en route, keeping an eye on the designated train time. If the fast train is significantly delayed or not due for ages, go to platform 3 for the slower train. Board the train and listen for the announcement that comes before it terminates at my destination. The fast train takes about 10 minutes with no prior stops; the slow one takes about 25 minutes with three prior stops. Get off the train, find the way out, done.

Big train stations are more problematic. The buildings are so big, and you cannot always find where you need to be quickly. There are more trains, more platforms, and the platform layout is more complicated, with some of them divided into A, B, and C. In London, there are many places where you have to scan your ticket and a maze of tunnels and staircases to navigate. When I say I feel like a small animal moving through a busy place, this is precisely the sort of environment I am thinking of! Very often, the station and the trains will be unbearably crowded. The fumes linger in your nose and throat with each breath, along with any sickly food smells and jumbled up scents of other people. This is where Vaseline or Tiger Balm come in handy. If you can tolerate the texture, gently smear them under your nose to mask other smells. While they won't eliminate unpleasant smells altogether, they will take the edge off them.

Aeroplanes

If there is one form of public transport I may never master unassisted, it's air travel. Airports are my kryptonite, despite having travelled by plane many times ever since I was a baby. They basically have all the worst elements of larger train stations with more paperwork to manage and more locations to check in with by a certain time. On top of that, the plane may get delayed by up to several hours, and you are advised to arrive well before your flight, meaning you are forced to put up with the overcrowding and sensory overload for a significant chunk of the day. Believe it or not, I like seeing different countries. I just find the process of getting there exhausting.

The Blue Band Scheme turned out to be a Godsend when I used it at Manchester Airport for my holiday in Spain in August 2016. I was given a wristband to use as proof of my autism so staff would know I was eligible for support. I couldn't help inwardly laughing at the fact that my supposedly blue band was, in fact, bright pink, but the main thing is that I got the help I needed, i.e. someone to follow and answer any questions once I said goodbye to my stepdad who had taken me to the airport. Once I arrived in Spain, I was escorted to where I met up with my grandad and his partner, who I was to be staying with. It was a tiring day, but it went about as smoothly as I could have hoped.

Perhaps more challenging was the mission trip abroad with my Christian discipleship group. I was nervous about the trip as a whole anyway, and this one was the first flight I had taken without any family members present at any stage. To give our leader an idea of the support I would need during the trip, my stepdad wrote a letter to him that included this extract:

> *"Grace has travelled by air a number of times but never unassisted. This trip will not be the time to break with that pattern! Just being part of a group does NOT count as assistance. Therefore, please note the following.*
>
> *Airports are nightmare places for people with autism because they bombard you with multiple messages by a variety of means, often simultaneously. Sometimes these messages are delivered with a lack of clarity and empathy by people who expect you already to know the general procedure.*
>
> *Grace needs clear, sensitive and discreet explanations through all stages of the airport process, from checking in to boarding the plane and finding the right seat, and then the whole thing in reverse at the destination airport. These explanations need to happen step by step as they become relevant, and preferably from only one person at any given moment. Just*

giving Grace (or any other autistic person) a list of instructions at the start is no good.

It will also be important to ensure that she is physically part of a group (or subgroup) at all times because she would struggle to know what to do or where to go on her own, even after getting through security. Regarding security, it is best to ensure that she is neither the first nor the last group member through so that there is support available if needed on both sides of the security area. Grace may struggle to process unexpected questions or instructions from airport staff. Having a familiar person keeping an eye so they can help if this happens would save Grace a lot of anxiety and confusion, especially if staff are not helpful."

Meanwhile, on the day of our flight, I had managed maybe a couple of hours of sleep on the floor at the house of some of the interns before meeting the whole group at 6:00 am at our taxi pick up spot. I was anxious, sleep-deprived, surrounded by people, and in an airport. The perfect recipe for an autistic shutdown! Our leader and the other interns were kind and helpful, but as we were taking off, something inside me snapped, and shutdown mode spiralled into a panic attack. Suddenly I was acutely aware that I was miles above the ground, unable to escape, being jolted around, surrounded by people, rapidly getting further away from my home and family, with the noise at an overpowering level and my ears in pain from the air pressure. I was sweating profusely but couldn't stop shaking. My heart was pounding, and I was feeling increasingly nauseous. When the people I was sitting with asked me if I was ok, I didn't have the mental capacity to respond. My fear of throwing up – especially in front of everyone – only added to my anxiety levels. As soon as we were allowed to get up, I went and hid in the nearest toilet cubicle. If I was going to be sick, at least I'd be away from the eyes of the other passengers.

Mercifully, shutting myself in a small, cool room away from everyone else seemed to be the antidote. Surprisingly, especially given the smell, I managed to ride out the anxiety without being sick. I gradually felt calm enough to return to my seat, but when we changed planes for the second part of our journey, the anxiety attack threatened to resurface, and I did not think I could face another flight. My friend who I was sitting with came to the rescue here. After praying for me, she then went on to chat to me about any topic of interest she could think of, and although I struggled to talk back at first, it really helped to distract me from how I was feeling.

Despite having been on a plane plenty of times before and since that day, I think I am more nervous while flying as a result. Although I don't dislike the actual flight as much as navigating the airport, I am very keenly aware of how high and fast a moving plane is. Unlike when in a car, you cannot stop and get out or even wind down the window. I realise this keeps oxygen levels at 100%, but it can have a similar effect on anxiety levels.

Public transport coping strategies:

As should be clear by now, navigating public transport has to be one of the least autism-friendly challenges out there (and there are a fair few of those!). How to manage it will depend on who you are with and what form of transport you are taking. Some basic points for most travel-related situations are:

- **Get an up-to-date timetable,** including information on how long your journey is likely to take.
- **Think about what you may find difficult so you can mentally prepare,** e.g. sensory overload, overcrowding, directions.
- If possible, **use the journey as an opportunity to recharge** and bring along a book, some earphones for listening to music, or anything else that will help you to relax.

- Think about **how to explain autistic struggles** to anyone you might ask for help, e.g. I am autistic, which means I need clear, concise communication given one to one; I may be easily overwhelmed by being in a busy, noisy place.
- If possible, **practise the journey with someone else** (I realise this is not possible for every form of transport but should be doable with short train or bus journeys).
- **Be mindful of your physical needs** during long journeys. Remember to **drink** so that you don't feel ill from dehydration. Have a small amount of **food** beforehand, as an empty stomach will be more easily irritated, and therefore more susceptible to travel sickness. Try to take opportunities to use the **toilet** when you can, if you can bring yourself to (I say this as someone who hates public toilets). Take any **travel sickness** remedies you need. **Dress** so that you are not too hot or too cold, ideally with layers that you can easily remove, put back on, and carry around.
- Similarly, **be mindful of your sensory needs** (again, especially during long journeys). Wear clothes that you will feel **comfortable** sitting in for long periods of time. If you need to, bring earphones to block out **noise** or dark glasses to filter **light**. To reduce unpleasant **smells** from food, chemicals, or people, try smearing something scented like Vaseline or Tiger Balm under your nose (as long as this won't worsen sensory overload!).

In short, be clear on what you need to know about your journey, travel with people who understand you and your needs (if you need to travel with anyone), and practise whatever form of self-care you need. Travel can be a complicated process. Why suffer any more than you have to?

CHAPTER 8

Bullying and Disrespectful Behaviour

> *"[...] As an autistic person, you face and overcome so many challenges every day. Even if you feel weak in the face of bullying, you are undeniably strong and resilient. No one is stronger than someone who faces the day and carries on despite feeling like an alien continuously."*
> – Naomi.

This is the kind of encouragement I could have done with at school and college. Unfortunately, bullying is an all-too-common problem for autistic and neurotypical people alike. I think this is largely due to too many unhappy people in the world – people who are jealous, angry, resentful, prejudiced, or insecure. Too often, they will have been conditioned to believe that they have to be in a position of power over others in order to have any worth.

When I was at college, there was this woman on my course – I think in her early to mid-20s at the time – who took an instant dislike to me. I'll call her Jade. My first encounter with Jade was when I was still packing up after a practical lesson after everyone else, and she came over and shouted at me for being so slow and holding everyone up. It didn't get any better from there. Practical lessons with her were a nightmare. If I were having trouble with any kind of physical work, she would laugh at me and imitate whatever I was failing at. I remember her sneering at me one cold day when I was struggling to walk on icy, uneven ground during an outdoor practical lesson. If I passed by her in the corridors, she would shove me or shout at me to move (see the picture at the beginning of the chapter). As you can probably gather, she was a bundle of laughs to work with. (She wasn't. That was sarcasm).

After a while, I got pretty good at ignoring Jade and carrying on with what I was doing regardless of her behaviour. What I wasn't so good at was actively trying to do something about it. I didn't fall to pieces in her presence, but I didn't stand up to her either. I didn't tell anyone in charge. As far as I was concerned, she wasn't going out of her way to pursue me, nor was she causing me any physical harm, so what was there to complain about?

Since then, I am lucky to have not experienced much bullying as an adult, but I am aware that many autistic adults still do. We come across differently to neurotypicals. We struggle with different things. We cannot always predict their behaviour or intentions, nor do we instinctively know how to respond to them. In a society that isn't always friendly to people who are different in any way, these things make us vulnerable.

But bullying isn't always as hard to eliminate as it might seem. Bullies maintain power by making other people feel small and scared, and the moment someone doesn't back down or highlights just how stupid the bullies' behaviour really is, that power starts to slip away. Below, Thomas gives another piece of advice that I wish I had heard when I was at college:

> *"The best way to deal with direct bullies that don't get out of your face is to ask them questions. [...] Drive the encounter to a logical level, keep your emotions in check and watch them fall apart when they actually have to engage their brain. [...] Develop your eye contact and lock in on them – even neurotypicals can find eye contact distressing if you hold it long enough."*

So with all that in mind, let's take a look at different forms of bullying and disrespectful behaviour and how to deal with them.[7,8]

Different types of bullying and how to deal with them

Form of bullying	**Examples**	**How to deal with it**
Physical	Kicking, hitting, shoving, throwing things, or doing anything else to cause physical pain, stealing or damaging belongings.	Stand up straight and give prolonged eye contact to make them uncomfortable, run or walk away before things escalate, calmly ask why they do those things.
Verbal	Name calling, teasing, insulting, mocking, belittling.	Calmly ask why they are saying those things, or if they are saying them to make themselves feel powerful, ignore it, firmly tell them to stop (ideally with prolonged eye contact), respond politely or humorously (as long as you don't think you're in any real danger).

Social	Spreading rumours and lies, alienating someone from other people, deliberately not including someone, gaslighting, trying to ruin someone's relationships with other people, doing or saying anything that will make the person look bad.	Carry on with your life as if you are unaffected (if at all possible), firmly correct any false claims, seek support from people who you trust not to get involved, look for new friends in a new social setting.
Prejudicial	Racism, sexism, ableism, homophobia, transphobia, anti-religion, discrimination against culture or social class. Note that prejudicial bullying tends to overlap with other forms of bullying.	Firmly correct any stereotypes or false assumptions, don't laugh at any racist/sexist (etc.) jokes and instead calmly explain that they are hurtful and not funny (even if the person meant well). If disrespectful behaviour is not explicitly prejudicial, but you think it comes from prejudice, ask the person why they are doing it, or if they would do it if you were white/male (etc.).[9]
Sexual	Sexual name calling, shaming someone because of how many/ few relationships they have had, inappropriate touching, insults or rude gestures about someone's body.	Ignore rude names, comments, or gestures, calmly ask why they are saying or doing those things, give prolonged eye contact if they touch you.

Cyber	Abusive comments, emails, and messages, online threats, sharing someone's personal details online, hacking into someone's email or social media accounts.	Take photos or screenshots of abusive comments and messages, don't delete them, don't reply to them, block the bully on any social media platform, report the bullying to the service/contact provider (e.g. Facebook), look up the Terms of Use for the service/contact provider for information on how to report harassment.[10]

And remember, when faced with any kind of bullying...

- **Make a note of the details of the bullying and report it if possible** – whether to someone at college or university, your employer, your family, or even the police if you are in real danger and you think they will take you seriously. If the bullying is at work, college, or university, there should be an anti-bullying/discrimination policy, which means that bullying will not be tolerated if authorities are aware of it.
- **Make sure you have a strong support system** so that you feel less alone. For most people, this will consist of friends and family.
- **Reach out to anyone else they are bullying,** if you know of anyone. If you can form a group, this may deter the bully.
- **Warn the bully** that action will be taken if the bullying continues. Use their name, remain firm and calm, and explain exactly what you plan to do if they keep bullying you.
- **Stand up to and/or report any bullying that happens to someone else** and make an effort to be there for that person.

- **Remember that the bully is probably a very angry, unhappy, insecure person** who may even have been the victim of mistreatment themselves. This doesn't justify their behaviour, but it can make them seem less scary and threatening if you remember this. As Thomas puts it:

  "Pity [bullies] in your head if needs be, just don't stoop to their level. Toss away the useless opinions in the trash. You don't need to fight them if they aren't getting in the way of your life or stepping over the boundaries. Be an adult, find your inner confidence, and view them as little insects buzzing around your head for no logical reason."

- **Try not to let the bullying change who you are for the worse.** This is how people often become bullies – through pent up anger, resentment, and feelings of powerlessness.

When disrespect is unintended

When I was doing my internship in the Christian bookshop, a customer asked me a lot of questions at once that I was struggling to make sense of, as customers often did. When trying to get him to clarify what he wanted, I told him I am autistic, and sometimes communication is confusing for me. And according to this man… I could ask God to heal me!

In that moment, what I really needed God to do was give me patience. And restore my faith in humanity.

There have been many situations in my life where I should have calmly but firmly stood up for myself. There have been significantly fewer where I actually have. This is one of them. I felt small and shaky on the inside, and I may have faltered a little, but I managed to explain that autism is not an illness to be cured, but rather a difference in the brain and that implying otherwise is actually rather hurtful. He got it in the end, and surrounding colleagues and customers were impressed. So clearly, I did something right.

This is just one example of how many microaggressions or displays of discrimination are not intended to be hurtful but simply come from ingrained bias or a lack of understanding. I have experienced this many times; for being autistic, for being half-Taiwanese, for being gay. For me, dealing with well-meaning but inappropriate questions and comments can be harder to deal with than bullying and hostility. With bullying, you have every right to ignore or report the person, but when they mean well, reacting with hostility will not help you or educate them. It is important to be able to respond openly and honestly, but respectfully too.

When people shout racial insults at me, for example, I ignore them and don't laugh at any jokes they make. They are being rude and deserve neither a reaction nor any respect. On the other hand, when a well-meaning person greets me by saying something like 'ni hao' (Chinese for hello), 'Konichiwa' (Japanese for hello), I try to be careful. It sets my teeth on edge because the other person has immediately made an assumption about my race in a way that they wouldn't if I were 100% white, and yet I know they didn't mean to. In this instance, I say, "I'm English." I will probably add that I don't like it when people stereotype me without getting to know me like any other person. I might also explain that I'm half Taiwanese but only speak English, am only in touch with the English side of my family and have lived in the UK since I was 4. I don't react with anger, but I don't turn a blind eye, either.

I have also had similar experiences with people making assumptions about autism. Some of these experiences were a source of inspiration for me when I was creating table 1 on people's reactions to you telling them you are autistic! One such experience was a conversation I had with a woman at church in which I mentioned I was autistic. She asked me if I had been to university. When I said I had, her next question was, "And what did you study? I bet it was Maths, Science, or IT!" One of the oldest autism assumptions under the sun. Apparently, she had known a few autistic people who were all experts in one of these subjects. I told her I had studied Creative Writing and Journalism and then explained that not all autistic people are the same and that it makes me uncomfortable when people make assumptions about me. She took it calmly enough, and that was the end of it. Again, no anger, just respectful honesty.

Finally, remember that you are also free to politely end the conversation any time if it is making you uncomfortable, especially if the other person is refusing to listen. You can just say 'I don't feel like talking about this anymore' and for most people, that will be enough.

Feeling patronised

This is a form of unintentional disrespect that I think needs its own section, given how commonly people with any kind of disability experience it. One of the things that I had no idea how to deal with at school was when people spoke to me as if I was a toddler. I would be muddling through a lesson as best I could. Most kids just ignored me, but there were always a few who would be trying to do stuff for me, explaining the simplest things, or telling the others 'it's not her fault she's slow'. Or weak. I even had one person ask me – completely innocently – if I had brain damage. Seriously.

It wasn't just kids either. I remember a teacher talking about our latest homework assignment and mentioning how I'd been allowed to skip certain parts because they were too hard. Or classroom assistants who would follow me like a shadow in front of other kids when all I needed was to ask a few extra questions.

What I found hard was knowing what to say. For the most part, I'd internalise the inner conflict between not wanting to offend and hating feeling patronised. Very occasionally, I'd speak up, but the other person would act like I'd just karate chopped them! So much for not offending.

This is a common struggle for people in any minority category. People who know little about said minority have no idea how to talk to us. Often, they get completely caught up in trying to make sense of whatever they do know. As a result, they often seem to forget to just get to know us the same way they would with anyone and to treat us differently only when we need it. And when being 'different' means we *do* need help in certain situations, it's hard to know how to communicate that when we don't want the other person to think we're helpless.

A common form of patronising is inspiration porn. Inspiration porn is when you read stories about people with physical disabilities, learning differences, etc., that portray them as being an example to everyone just for getting through life with their condition. Maybe they're shown doing a normal activity that may or may not be harder for them, leaving everyone amazed that they managed it at all. Or they need help or friendship, someone offers it, and suddenly that person is seen as a saint. It seems that everything the disabled person does is either because of or in spite of their disability.

Now I understand these reactions are well meant. There *are* neurotypical based skills that are harder to manage when you are on the spectrum. Showing kindness to an autistic person *is* a good thing. But there will be many things in our lives that are just routine to us and/or are unrelated to our autism. We don't exist solely to inspire others by managing these things. Like pity, when someone showers us with praise over the smallest thing, it implies that they don't expect us to be that capable.

I once read an article that claimed that disabled people are here to educate typically abled people. Well, thank you, typically abled writer, for giving me, and others like me, a purpose in life. I don't know what we would do without people like you to be a learning tool for – maybe find our own set of goals and work towards them because they are important to us? No, surely nothing that outrageous.

Those last three sentences were sarcasm, by the way.

I *do* want to raise autism understanding among neurotypical people through talking and writing about it, but I do so because life would be easier for us on the spectrum if more people understood. Not because it is the only purpose I'll ever have.

As a side note, I should probably differentiate between validating someone's struggles and achievements and inspiration porn. We all survive tough times and accomplish things that we're proud of. I certainly appreciate it when people understand my struggles and admire my achievements. I just don't like feeling as if I exist purely to make neurotypical people feel good. I appreciate admiration as much as anyone, but I want to earn it through genuine accomplishments. Not through getting out of bed and facing the day like everyone else.

The thing to remember is that most people who accidentally patronise us have the best of intentions. If they are trying to help, they probably want to do the right thing. It's hard to know where to draw the line between politely but firmly explaining yourself and sounding unfriendly or ungrateful. If you have autism – just like any other condition that puts you in a minority – chances are, you do have different needs that require accommodation. That doesn't mean you cannot do things for yourself. Don't wait until you feel like exploding with frustration. You can explain to the other person what you don't need as well as what you do need. If the person reacts to this negatively, then that can be hard to deal with, but that is their problem, and it doesn't take away your right to speak for yourself. Below, I have created a table of different forms of patronising and possible ways to respond. You may come up with your own. If so, definitely make a note of them!

How to respond to being patronised

Forms of patronising	How to respond
Talking to someone else about you in front of you.	You can talk directly to me. If [the other person] wants or needs to join in, they will.
Talking more loudly and/or slowly.	You don't need to talk more loudly/slowly. If I need you to be clearer about something, I will ask.
Talking to you as if you are a child.	I'm still an adult, like any other in most ways, and I appreciate it when people talk to me like an adult. OR (if the same person keeps doing it) I appreciate that you are trying to get it right, but when people talk to me like that, it makes me feel like they forget that I'm an adult like any other in most ways.
Pitying you just because you are autistic.	It sounds like you pity me for being autistic. If so, you don't need to. It's not a lesser way of being, it just means my brain works differently in some ways.

Constantly trying to help unnecessarily.	Thank you, but if I need any help, I will ask for it. OR (if the same person keeps doing it) I understand that you want to help, and I appreciate that, but when you assume I need help with everything, it makes me feel like you don't expect me to be that capable. If I need any help, I will ask for it.
Praising you for the smallest things.	Thank you, but that was no more difficult for me than for anyone else. OR (if the same person keeps doing it) I understand that you want to be kind, and I appreciate that, but when you praise me for things that aren't difficult, it makes me feel like you don't expect me to be that capable.
Thinking you are inspirational just for getting through life with autism.	Thanks, but I'd far rather inspire people by the way I treat others/ the things I've worked for and achieved, not for my mere existence.
Thinking autistic people (or disabled/neurodivergent people in general) exist to teach and/or inspire typically abled people.	I exist as an individual in my own right, just like everyone else.

In short, not all disrespectful behaviours are an expression of hostility. Sometimes the hardest interactions to deal with are with people who say something ignorant or insensitive with good intentions. Explaining how it makes you feel may be uncomfortable for the other person – and you – but doing so calmly and respectfully may give them the opportunity to understand and learn.

Conclusion

When writing a blog post (at unwrittengrace.wordpress.com), I have often found the beginning and the ending to be the hardest bits. This has definitely proven true for this book. From childhood until only very recently, it seemed like nothing more than a nice idea. It was fun to dream about, but making it happen? Who did I think I was kidding?

Incidentally, when I was at college, I remember finding several Special Educational Needs leaflets in the library, including one about Asperger's Syndrome. It depicted the classic stereotype of autistic people never being able to understand other people and their emotions. I decided to take matters into my own hands and write my own version, which I offered to the Learner Support staff. They fobbed me off by saying, well done, they weren't sure about replacing the original, but maybe I should write a book one day! Eleven years later, here we are…

Now, as I think of how best to wrap it up, I find myself looking back on all I have learned from my experiences and also from all the reflecting and processing that writing this book has forced me to do. I have had to find the strength to speak up about certain issues that may make some neurotypicals uncomfortable. I have had to do some serious introspection to understand my emotions and needs, how I might express them, and, where applicable, what bad experiences may have caused them so I can find the words to address these issues.

Through research, I have learned many things about how autism is seen that have saddened or angered me. Some people do not take our intelligence seriously when they find out we are autistic; others do not take our struggles seriously if and when we appear neurotypical. I have read about people ranting about how we shouldn't be romanticising autism (I'm not; I'm trying to spread understanding and acceptance). I have found many online autism resources by neurotypicals who speak of us with condescending compassion. Some books people have given to me in the past make autistic people sound like hopeless cases with no emotions. I have come across fictional and non-fictional stories that use autistic characters only as a learning tool, plot device, or source of inspiration porn for non-autistic characters and readers. All of these issues have boosted my motivation on days when the mere sight of my unfinished manuscript has made me feel sick. However, while I hope never to stop caring, I have had to learn to be patient with the rest of the world.

One thing I have learned through my experiences of being autistic – and gay and mixed race – is that we are all a bit the same and a bit different. If I think of myself and any other person in my life, I could spend all day analysing our similarities and our differences. In the case of autistic and neurotypical people, we feel and react to things differently. We express ourselves differently. We take a different approach to learning, communicating, and getting things done. At the same time, we all have the capacity to feel. We all have things we are good at and not so good at. We all make mistakes. We all have complex personalities that are a mix of our biology and our upbringing. When looking at different groups of people, it is easy to either fixate on their differences or dismiss these as unimportant. But real life isn't that black and white, and we might as well try to remember that.

So on that note, let me go through a few other things that I hope you, the reader, will take away from this book.

If you are not autistic:

1) Thank you for reading this book! In doing so, you have taken a step towards understanding autism from the inside.

Keep looking for resources by autistic people. Autism resources written by and for neurotypicals aren't necessarily wrong, but be aware that they usually only give an outsider's perspective and sometimes contradict what autistic people say. To spread autism understanding and acceptance, please amplify what autistic people are saying.

2) If an autistic person says something is hard, please do not try to convince them otherwise just because it isn't hard for you. Non-verbal social cues often do not come naturally to us. Eye contact makes it harder for us to listen. Many of us experience certain sensory stimuli way more intensely than most people. We are trying pretty damn hard to get by in a world where we are outnumbered by people of a different neurotype, so please bear with us!

3) Know the difference between reprimanding us for things we do or say that are actually problematic and reprimanding us for things we do or say that are simply a bit 'autistic'. Being autistic isn't an inferior way of being, but neither does it mean that we cannot take responsibility for our mistakes. If we say or do something that is offensive, you have every right to say so in a concise, logical manner.

4) Don't let the autism stereotypes and tales of woe scare you. The autistic community is a pretty diverse bunch with a wide range of talents, flaws, and personalities – just like you neurotypicals!

And if you are autistic:

1) The obvious one: being different does not equal being lesser. Remember that many of our so-called 'deficits' are only described as such because they do not fit the neurotypical standard. Your strengths, weaknesses, and personal interests are not inappropriate (well, unless they cause harm to you or

others). Your social skills are not worse than neurotypicals'. They are just different. You are not broken or sick and do not let the majority tell you otherwise. Just keep following the road less travelled and see where it takes you.

2) Being different can be bloody exhausting, and there is no shame in admitting that. Hiding any part of your identity chips away at your soul. Openly being yourself requires enough bravery to shed any internalised shame and enough patience to take other people's reactions in your stride. But all these challenges can give you a strength you might not have otherwise found. And there will be more people who are similar to you than you think. Find them, get to know them, and have fun being yourself without having to explain anything!

3) It's ok to grow and move forward in your own time. Tell people about your autism when you feel ready. Learn to be at peace with being single until you find a relationship. Don't feel pressured to go to college or university at the same time as everyone else – or even at all. You may find your ideal job after a few weeks, or months, or years. There will be some times in your life when you overcome many challenges and others when you settle for years without much change. Clichéd, I know, but it's important to remember and easy to forget.

4) You deserve to be heard, understood, and respected. This is the same whether you have low or high support needs, whether you are speaking, non-speaking, or anywhere in between, whether or not you are officially diagnosed, whether or not you also have physical disabilities or other neurological disabilities, and whatever your gender, sexuality, race, colour, or culture.

Finally, autistic and neurotypical readers alike, for the love of all that is good… don't get caught in possession. Sorry, couldn't resist. Now get out there and spread some autism understanding!

Glossary of Metaphors and Idioms in this Book

At all costs – another way of saying 'no matter what'.

At arm's length – to keep someone at arm's length means to not get too close to them, physically, emotionally, or both.

Came to a head – when a situation comes to a head, it means it has reached a point where it becomes clear that something needs to change.

Cat-fished – to catfish someone means to lure them into a relationship by creating a false online persona.

Closet – being 'in the closet' usually refers to not having told anyone that you are LGBTQA (+). '**Coming out of the closet**' or simply '**coming out**' refers to telling people. In the first chapter, I also used this phrase to mean telling people about being autistic.

Coined – to have invented a new word or phrase.

Draw the line – set a limit for what is acceptable in any given situation.

Eyes of a hawk – very good at seeing and noticing things. To watch someone/something with the eyes of a hawk means to observe them very carefully.

Feel more human – to feel better or more normal.

Fighting their way to the top of the social hierarchy – trying to have the most power and influence in a social setting.

Gel with – to gel with someone means to get on with them quickly and easily.

Get one thing straight – to make something perfectly clear; to do away with any uncertainty.

Get your butt out of there – to leave somewhere quickly.

Ground-breaking – surprising, extraordinary.

In the thick of – to be in the thick of a situation means to be in the worst stage of it.

Keeping my head above water – to keep your head above water means to just about avoid getting overwhelmed by a difficult situation.

Kryptonite – something that is particularly bad for the wellbeing of the person or thing in question.

Mixed bag – a mix of good and bad.

Road less travelled – to take the road less travelled means to live in a way or make a choice that is less common than the alternative.

Rule of thumb – a personal rule to go by in a certain situation if in doubt.

Sets my teeth on edge – if something sets your teeth on edge, that means it annoys you or makes you really uncomfortable.

Skyrocketed – to have increased dramatically.

Slip under the radar – to go unnoticed.

Soak up emotions like a sponge – to be very keenly aware of how other people are feeling to the point where you feel it too.

Takes guts – requires courage.

Take the edge off – to make something less intense or unpleasant.

Through the roof – when something is said to be through the roof, it has reached extremely high levels.

True colours – one's natural personality and behaviour.

Train of thought – a sequence of thoughts and ideas.

Turn a blind eye – to turn a blind eye means to pretend not to notice something.

Vouch for – to confirm something that has been said about a person, thing, or situation.

Walking on eggshells – feel like you have to be overly careful not to offend someone or cause trouble.

Wearing thin – if something is said to be wearing thin, that means it is losing its appeal.

Where you stand with each other – to know where you stand with someone means to have a rough idea of how they feel about you and how it is appropriate to behave around them.

Wrap it up – to neatly finish a task.

Sources Referred to in the Text

1) Autism West Midlands (2016) *Meltdown and shutdown in people with autism*. Available at: https://www.autismwestmidlands.org.uk/wp-content/uploads/2017/11/Meltdown_shutdown.pdf (Accessed: 12 June 2020)

2) Witton, H. (2020) *Doing It! With Hannah Witton – Autism, Dating and Relationships with Thomas Henley.* Available at: https://pod.link/doingit/episode/015ed18f0e2bea0611998ff9f4038d27 (Accessed: 1 March 2021)

3) Henley, T. (2020) *Different Wavelengths - Dating An Autistic Ep.1 (Love On The Spectrum)*. Available at: https://www.youtube.com/watch?v=EyJc0vBwL7A&list=PLgrPK8ttTCY29tIzkHi4zc5ob_nXerJLJ 12 August (Accessed: 1 March 2021)

4) Booth, J. (2016) *Autism Equality in the Workplace*. London: Jessica Kingsley Publishers

5) Scope.org (no date) *Support with problems at work.* Available at: https://www.scope.org.uk/advice-and-support/work-careers/support-with-problems-at-work/ (Accessed: 20 June 2021)

6) Booth, J. (2016) *Autism Equality in the Workplace*. London: Jessica Kingsley Publishers

7) Mukherjee, C. (2021) *Different Types of Bullying.* Available at: https://themindfool.com/different-types-of-bullying/#Bullying_Definition (Accessed: 1 May 2021)

8) LaMotte, S. (2019) *How to handle the adult bully in your life.* Available at: https://edition.cnn.com/2019/09/20/health/adult-bully-survivor-tips-wellness/index.html (Accessed: 1 May 2021)

9) Adenle, C. (2020) *12 Effective Ways to Deal with Racism at Work.* Available at: https://catherinescareercorner.com/2020/07/22/12-effective-ways-to-deal-with-racism-at-work/ (Accessed: 1 May 2021)

10) Patchin, J. (2015) *Advice for Adult Victims of Cyberbullying.* Available at: https://cyberbullying.org/advice-for-adult-victims-of-cyberbullying (Accessed: 1 May 2021)

Other Relevant Resources

The following resources can provide information and support for autistic people and their families. They are UK based unless otherwise specified:

The Advisory Conciliation and Arbitration Service (ACAS)

Acas.org.uk

An organisation dedicated to giving free, impartial advice on rights and rules in the workplace. For their equality and diversity section, please go to: https://www.acas.org.uk/about-us/equality-and-diversity-at-acas

Aspergers Growth YouTube Channel

Thomas Henley's YouTube Channel, where you can find his documentary Aspergers in Society, the Thoughty Auti podcast (see below), and many other autism related videos.

Autistic Inclusive Meets (AIM)

Autisticinclusivemeets.org

An organisation dedicated to promoting autism acceptance and supporting autistic people and their families.

Autistic Nottingham

Autisticnottingham.org

An autistic led charity based in Nottingham, UK, dedicated to supporting autistic adults with lower support needs.

Autistic UK

Autisticuk.org

An autistic led network seeking to encourage autistic inclusion and self-advocacy.

Autistic Women & Nonbinary Network (AWN)

Awnnetwork.org

An organisation in Nebraska, USA, providing community, support, and information for autistic women, transgender, and non-binary people.

Chris Bonnello

Chrisbonnello.com

Autisticnotweird.com

Autistic writer, novelist, public speaker, special needs tutor, and blogger at Autistic not weird.

In The Loop About Neurodiversity

Intheloopaboutneurodiversity.wordpress.com

Blog based in Oregon, USA, that promotes neurodiversity acceptance and representation.

Laurie Morgen

Lauriemorgen.co.uk

Autistic public speaker and author of *Travelling by Train – The Journey of an Autistic Mother*.

My Legal Advisor

Mylegaladvisor.co.uk

An online legal marketplace that enables consumers and businesses to find a lawyer. For information about disability discrimination at work, please go to https://mylegaladviser.co.uk/advice/discrimination-at-work.

The National Autistic Society

Autism.org.uk

The UK's leading autism charity, which promotes information and support for autistic people and their families. For their section on employment, please go to https://www.autism.org.uk/what-we-do/employment/autism-at-work. For their section on driving, please go to: https://www.autism.org.uk/advice-and-guidance/topics/transport/driving. If you would like to see my interview on their *Stories from the Spectrum* page, please go to https://www.autism.org.uk/advice-and-guidance/stories/stories-from-the-spectrum-grace-liu.

Neurodivergent Rebel

Neurodivergentrebel.com

LGBTQA (+) autistic YouTuber, blogger, and manager at Neurodivergent Consulting, based in Texas, USA.

Thomas Henley

Thomashenley.co.uk

Thomas Henley's website with information about autism and mental health, and links to his YouTube channel and podcast.

The Thoughty Auti podcast

Thomas Henley's podcast featuring autistic people from various backgrounds talking about topics relating to autism and mental health (I'm on episode 17). Available on YouTube, Anchor, Spotify, Apple podcasts, Podcast Addict, and Thomas' website.

Unwrittengrace

Unwrittengrace.wordpress.com

My blog, in which I regularly write about my thoughts and experiences as an autistic person. I also write about intersectionality, entertaining life anecdotes, and other topics of interest.

About the Author

Grace Liu has been blogging about autism since 2013. She has written several articles for the National Autistic Society and the magazine and website of the university where she studied. She has also appeared on the Thoughty Auti podcast and the Potty Mouth podcast. Grace lives in the Midlands of England with her parents and three cats.

Blog: Unwrittengrace.wordpress.com

Facebook page: Unwritten Grace – autism and writing

Instagram: unwrittengraceblogs

Twitter: unwrittengracel